fP

NO LIMITS

The Will to Succeed

MICHAEL PHELPS

WITH ALAN ABRAHAMSON

FREE PRESS

New York   London   Toronto   Sydney

FREE PRESS
A Division of Simon & Schuster, Inc.
1230 Avenue of the Americas
New York, NY 10020

First Free Press hardcover edition December 2008

FREE PRESS and colophon are trademarks of Simon & Schuster, Inc.

For information about special discounts for bulk purchases,
please contact Simon & Schuster Special Sales at
1-800-456-6798 or business@simonandschuster.com

DESIGNED BY ERICH HOBBING

Manufactured in the United States of America

1   3   5   7   9   10   8   6   4   2

Library of Congress Control No.: 2008044696

ISBN-13: 978-1-4391-3072-8
ISBN-10:   1-4391-3072-8

To the power of dreams

*Special thanks to my family, coach, teammates,
and numerous others who helped me reach my goals
—Michael*

*To Kayla, Bobby, and Rachel
—Alan*

CONTENTS

NO
LIMITS

PROLOGUE

I screamed. You bet I did. I mean, I totally let loose. I clenched my fist and arched my back and screamed and howled and yelled.

And it felt so good. So very good.

No, it felt great.

Better, maybe. It was primal. It was as good as it gets.

I let it all out: joy, relief, excitement, passion, and pride, especially pride in being an American.

It's like that at the Olympic Games. Years of training, of hard work, of desire and discipline—all of it compressed into minutes, sometimes just seconds, and time seems to stand still as history plays itself out.

There's nothing sweeter than winning.

And we had just won. We had set a world record, too, obliterated the old record, really. The Stars and Stripes. The American men. Us.

I had just been part of, had also just been witness to, the most amazing, thrilling, exciting, supercharged swimming race ever, an instant classic if ever there was one, one of the greatest moments in Olympic history.

Even before the start of the race that morning, the atmosphere inside the Water Cube in Beijing, the swimming and diving venue at the 2008 Summer Games, was electric, the noise ferocious.

This was the 400-meter freestyle relay. Four guys on each team. Each swims two laps of the pool.

Eight lanes in the pool, eight teams, but really only three that were likely to win: the Americans, the French, the Australians.

I went first. Garrett Weber-Gale followed. Cullen Jones followed him. And then came Jason Lezak, our anchor.

When Jason dove in, the French were slightly, ever so slightly, ahead.

Halfway through his leg, Jason, who has for years been one of the truly outstanding sprinters in the entire world, one of the best freestyle relay swimmers ever, had fallen farther behind the French racer, Alain Bernard, who had come into the relay as the world-record holder in the 100.

With 30 meters to go, Jason was behind.

With 20 to go, he was still behind.

But he was charging.

Now Jason was gaining.

On the deck, we were going crazy, Garrett and I. Not that anyone could hear us. It was so loud inside the Water Cube that you couldn't hear yourself think. Not that anyone was thinking. We were wishing, hoping, praying, urging. Shouting, screaming, yelling. Come on, Jason! Get that guy! Get him! Get that guy! Get him!

At the wall, Jason reached out his hand. We turned to look at the big board across the pool and—yes!

Jason had done it! He had, somehow, done it!

Jason had thrown down the fastest relay leg of all time. We needed every bit of that. We had won, the scoreboard said, by eight-hundredths of a second. The French were second, the Australians third.

I had no words. I had only screams.

Because this was not about me.

It was epic.

Of course I had won a gold medal, and that was the goal. But

PROLOGUE

this was about something way bigger than any personal accomplishment. We swam together, competed together, four as one, together, as a team and as Americans.

But that only begins to explain why I had no words.

Of course the relay gold kept alive my quest to chase eight gold medals at a single Olympics. I understood that then even as I understand it now, as I will understand it always.

But that was not why I had no words. The notion of eight golds was always a means to an end. It was never about chasing fame or fortune or celebrity.

Never.

If I could win eight, could go one better than the great Mark Spitz and the seven golds he won at the Munich Olympics in 1972, those eight medals might do what nothing else could. They could help to make real my biggest dream, to elevate swimming's place in the American sports landscape, and to make it an every-year sport instead of a once-every-four-years sport.

I never set out to be the second Mark Spitz.

I only wanted to be the first Michael Phelps.

I wanted to do something no one had ever done before.

Baseball is great, basketball so cool, football so fine; I love the NFL, especially my Baltimore Ravens. But in other countries, particularly Australia, swimming has the same cachet that baseball, basketball, and football have in the United States, with packed houses and passionate fans. Why can't it be like that in the United States?

It can.

That's why, when Jason touched first, I had no words.

A few days later, I found myself again without words, after I swam my last race at the 2008 Summer Games, the 400-meter medley relay. Aaron Peirsol went first, swimming the backstroke; Brendan Hansen swam the breaststroke; I swam the third leg, the butterfly; and then, just as he had done in the 400 free relay, Jason brought us home in first, this time ahead of the Australians.

3

We had done it, another gold.

I had won eight gold medals.

I let out another scream. I thanked my teammates, and a jumble of emotions washed over and around me. I felt gratitude and relief and joy, just sheer joy at the moment, at the culmination of a journey filled with twists and turns and ups and downs. I felt humbled, too. I felt profound humility at learning how I had become a source of inspiration for so many back home, everyone who said I offered renewed proof that America and Americans could still take on the world with courage and grit, who declared that the virtues so many Americans hold so dear—hard work, character, commitment to family, team, and country—could still triumph.

No matter where Americans were in the world, I'd been told, they were watching and cheering; that was special. Back home, I'd heard, bars were erupting in cheers when I'd won. I'd heard that my races had been shown on jumbo video screens at Major League Baseball and NFL games, on one of those big screens in Times Square. I understood that the drama and anticipation and excitement of some of my races had kept people glued to their television sets into the night. That very first relay. The 200-meter butterfly, when my goggles filled with water and I couldn't see, literally couldn't see, and still won. And then the 100-meter butterfly, which I had won by one-hundredth of a second.

I looked into the stands, for my mom, Debbie, and my sisters, Whitney and Hilary. When I found them, I walked through a horde of photographers and climbed into the stands to give each of them a kiss, with the memories of where we'd been and what we'd overcome flooding over me. Mom put her arm around my neck and gave me an extra hug.

When I was in grade school, I was diagnosed with attention deficit/hyperactivity disorder, or ADHD. I had overcome that. When I was in school, a teacher said I'd never be successful.

Things like that stick with you and motivate you; I flashed back to that with my family there in the stands. I started crying. My mom started crying. My sisters started crying.

I started swimming when I was a little boy. Both Hilary and Whitney were champion swimmers, and when I was very much the baby brother, it looked like Whitney was the one from our family who was going to make it to the Olympics. That didn't happen. And here I was.

I felt lucky for the talent that I have, the drive that I have, the want, the excitement about the sport, felt lucky for every quality I have, and have worked so hard to have. In some sports, you can excel if you have natural talent. Not in swimming. You can have all the talent in the world, be built just the right way, but you can't be good or get good without hard work. In swimming, there's a direct connection between what you put into it and what you get out of it.

I knew I would find my coach and longtime mentor, Bob Bowman, around the pool deck. Bob, the only coach I've ever had. He had trained me, punished me, motivated me, inspired me, and proven to me the connection between hard work and success. Bob has long been one of the very few people in my life to tell me the unadulterated truth, even when I didn't want to listen. Perhaps most important, especially when I didn't want to hear it.

Bob's philosophy is rather simple: We do the things other people can't, or won't, do. Bob's expectations are simple, too. It's like the quote he had up on the whiteboard one day at practice a few months before the Games. It comes from a business book but in sports it's the same: "In business, words are words, explanations are explanations, promises are promises, but only performance is reality."

Bob is exquisitely demanding. But it is with him that I learned this essential truth: Nothing is impossible.

And this: Because nothing is impossible, you have to dream big dreams; the bigger, the better.

So many people along the way, whatever it is you aspire to do, will tell you it can't be done. But all it takes is imagination.

You dream. You plan. You reach.

There will be obstacles. There will be doubters. There will be mistakes.

But with hard work, with belief, with confidence and trust in yourself and those around you, there are no limits. Perseverance, determination, commitment, and courage—those things are real. The desire for redemption drives you. And the will to succeed—it's everything. That's why, on the pool deck in Beijing in the summer of 2008, there were sometimes no words, only screams.

Because, believe it, dreams really can come true.

1

PERSEVERANCE:
THE 400 INDIVIDUAL MEDLEY

Leading up to and through the 2008 U.S. Olympic Trials for swimming, which were held in Omaha, Nebraska, in late June and early July, I kept having a most particular dream.

It involved the number 3:07.

The 2008 Summer Games in Beijing would get under way on August 8. I had no idea what 3:07 meant, or why, or why I kept dreaming about it.

But, there it was: 3:07.

Logically, naturally, it seemed like a time.

But a time for what?

3:07 in the afternoon? In the morning?

I am a fanatic for training and for hard work and discipline. Even so, I wasn't getting up at 3:07 in the morning to go to the pool, that was for sure.

I couldn't figure it out.

It was especially perplexing because swimming, like baseball or football, is a sport with its own history and lore that lends itself elegantly to numbers and statistics.

Everyone who follows baseball knows that Babe Ruth hit 714 home runs during his career, for instance, or that Ted Williams hit .406 in 1941, or that Bob Gibson pitched so magnificently in 1968 that he ended the year with an ERA of 1.12.

Everyone who knows a thing or two about football knows that the Miami Dolphins went 17–0 in 1972, or that Tom Brady threw fifty touchdown passes during the 2007 NFL season.

Even people who don't know much about swimming almost surely know that Mark Spitz won seven gold medals in 1972 at the Olympic Games in Munich. And that I could win eight in Beijing in 2008. Eight is an auspicious number in Chinese culture. The Games were going to start on 8/8/08, at precisely 8:00 p.m. local time; the date and time were picked because the Chinese word for eight, *ba*, sounds like the word for prosperity, *fa*.

The problem I was having, though, was simple. There is nothing in swimming in which 3:07 made any sense whatsoever, which was totally weird, because there are vast columns of numbers in swimming to crunch. The sport is measured mostly in meters but sometimes in yards. There are world records, Olympic records, American records, even what are called U.S. Open records, meaning a mark that is set on American soil, whether by an American or someone from somewhere else.

The swim calendar in recent years has kept to a fairly consistent routine, too, at least for American swimmers, which makes it all the easier to track the numbers: meets early in the year in places as different as Long Beach, California, and Columbia, Missouri; in May or June in Santa Clara, California; and one or two major meets, such as the U.S. Nationals, the Pan Pacific Championships, the swimming world championships, and, every fourth summer, the Olympics.

Moreover, I can, at a given moment, pretty much rattle off times for the events I swim, in either yards or meters.

In none of those columns of records did 3:07 compute.

Still, the dream kept coming.

3:07.

When I'm in training, as I was before the 2008 Olympics in Ann Arbor, Michigan, where I had moved after growing up near Baltimore, we typically practice early in the morning, then again in the late afternoon at the University of Michigan's Canham Natatorium. In between, I usually take a nap.

We would swim miles in the morning, then more miles in the afternoon.

Eat. Swim. Do other workouts, like weightlifting. Sleep. That was the routine. Believe me, working out that hard in the morning and then again in the afternoon made a nap no luxury. It was an essential.

One of the things about my naps is this: If I'm sitting there right before I doze off or immediately after I get up, I can visualize how I want the perfect race to go. I can see the start, the strokes, the walls, the turns, the finish, the strategy, all of it. It's so vivid that I can vividly see incredible detail, down even to the wake behind me.

It's my imagination at work, and I have a big imagination. Visualizing like this is like programming a race in my head, and that programming sometimes seems to make it happen just as I had imagined it.

I can also visualize the worst race, the worst circumstances. That's what I do to prepare myself for what might happen. It's a good thing to visualize the bad stuff. It prepares you. Maybe you dive in and your goggles fill with water. What do you do? How do you respond? What is important right now? You have to have a plan.

I'm not really sure, precisely, why I'm able to visualize like this. I have always been able to do it, ever since I was little. It's also true that I got lots of practice growing up; since I've been swimming it's been very much a part of the rhythm and routine of my life and of the house in which I grew up.

I grew up the baby brother in a house rumbling with girl power. My sister Whitney is five years older than I am, Hilary seven. When she was little, Hilary wanted to be the next Janet Evans, the record-setting American swimmer who was perhaps the best female distance swimmer of all time; Janet won five Olympic medals, four gold, between the 1988 and 1992 Games. Hilary grew up to be an excellent distance swimmer and set records at the University of Richmond. Whitney, as a teenager, was one of the best butterfly swimmers in the United States; she competed at the 1996 Olympic Trials.

So I was always, always around the pool. When I was a baby, my mom used to pick me up out of my crib, my pajamas still on, and drive me and the girls to the North Baltimore Aquatic Club (NBAC) at the Meadowbrook Aquatic and Fitness Center. She would change me in the car and, while the girls were swimming laps, I would stay there and play.

The North Baltimore club has a tradition of excellence, including female gold medalists at the 1984, 1992, and 1996 Olympics, and training there included sessions during which kids were taught how to visualize, as part of the process of setting goals. Whitney remembers it like it was yesterday. Sit quietly in a room, lights down, see a race from start to finish: diving in, how and when to breathe, what it would feel like to turn hard off the wall, to power to the finish, even how to get out of the pool.

Mom and I used to go through relaxation and programming techniques at home. My coach, Bob Bowman, had my mom buy a book that set out drills and exercises, including one in which I would tighten my right hand into a fist and relax it, then do the same with my left hand, as a way of learning to deal with tension. At night, before falling asleep, I would lie on my bed and she would read to me from that book, and I would practice.

When I was thirteen or fourteen, Bob started asking me to play a race in my head as though it were a video. When we were in training, we'd get to the last repetition of a set, particularly a really hard set, and Bob would want me to do that last repeat close to race speed. He'd say, okay, put in the tape and see yourself, for instance, swimming the 400 individual medley at the nationals.

To this day, if Bob says, okay, put in the videotape, that's what he means.

They say that the mental aspect of sports is just as important as the physical part. There can be no doubt about that: Being mentally tough is critical. At an Olympic final, you know everybody has physical talent. So, who's going to win? The mentally toughest. Bob is a big believer in that. I am, too. Bob also believes that my visualization skills carry over to my training, and to my racing, and that it's part of what makes me different.

Bob and I have been together for so long—we started together when I was eleven, and I turned twenty-three during the 2008 Trials, in Omaha—that he doesn't even have to say much to me now to make sure I'm preparing mentally as well as physically.

He doesn't have to nag. Not like that would work.

He just says something like, how's the visualizing going?

Fine, I'll say.

Or, he'll say, have you started yet?

Yes, I'll say. Or, not yet. Whatever. Bob just wants to make sure it's happening.

It always happens. Always.

But nothing was leading me to the answer of what my dream meant.

3:07. I kept trying to figure out the mystery.

An Olympic-sized pool is 50 meters long.

I don't swim the 50-meter freestyle sprint in competition. But I knew, of course, that whoever was going to win the sprint at the Beijing Olympics would do so, given advancements in pool technology and in swimsuits, in particular the Speedo LZR Racer, in well under 22 seconds.

The 100-meter freestyle winner would go in about 47 seconds. The 200 free would end in about 1 minute, 43 seconds, the 400 free in about 3:42, maybe slightly under.

There are three other strokes on the Olympic program: the backstroke, the breaststroke, and the butterfly. But races in those two strokes are only at 100 and 200 meters, not anywhere near long enough to be in the water for 3:07.

There are three relays on the Olympic program, too. Two of them are freestyle relays, the 400 and the 800. Four swimmers take turns swimming laps, 100 meters apiece in the 400, 200 apiece in the 800. In neither of those could 3:07 mean anything.

The other relay is what's called the 400 medley relay. Again, four swimmers take turns swimming laps. In the medley each swims a different stroke: in order, the backstroke, breaststroke, butterfly, freestyle. The winning time in the medley tends to be about three and a half minutes.

I was completely stumped.

Finally, I went to Bob to ask him what he thought it might be. Bob usually has the answers. It can be frustrating but it's true: Bob usually has the answers.

Bob's interests out of the pool range across a wide variety of subjects. He can tell you about thoroughbred horses. About the architecture of Frank Lloyd Wright. About the genius of Beethoven's Ninth Symphony. Bob played violin and went to Florida State because it was an excellent music school; he studied music composition very seriously. He then switched to child psychology. Bob gets asked all the time if I see a sports psychologist. He answers: every day.

The dynamic of our relationship over the years has been this: Bob pushed. I pushed right back. Bob can be gruff. He can be demanding. Sometimes he yells at me; as I've gotten older, I've shouted right back. The venting we do at each other just shows that I'm not scared of him, and he is for sure not scared of me. And the vast majority of the time, as in any partnership that works, and ours works, totally, we get along great. Because, bottom line, Bob is not only coach and mentor but so much more.

When I was younger, he had taught me how to tie a tie. For my first school dance, when I was thirteen, he let me leave practice fifteen minutes early; when I showed up with the tie and went to put it on, he noticed that my shirt was buttoned one button off. So we fixed that together. When I was a teenager, he taught me how to drive. His car was a stick shift, and that's how I learned. I always had trouble: I remember going to school one day, on a hill at a busy intersection, and of course I stalled the car in the middle of the hill. There were tons of people behind me. We fixed that together, too. I remember getting out of a workout and going to the prom—regular black tux, stretch white Hummer limo—and Bob was there to watch me head off.

All the little things like that: Bob has always been there for me.

At the Trials, I told Bob, I'm trying to make sense of this 3:07. What do you think it could be?

At first, he said he didn't know.

The only thing he could think of, he finally said, was that 3:07 somehow related to the 400 individual medley, a race that like the medley relay combines all four strokes. The difference, of course, is that it's just one person doing all the swimming, not four. Also, the order is different from the medley relay. In the IM, it goes: fly, back, breast, free.

I had held the world record in the 400 IM since 2002. When I first set the record, at the summer nationals in Fort Lauderdale, Florida, I touched in 4:11.09. Over the years, I had lowered the record a number of other times. At the 2007 world championships in Melbourne, Australia, I had lowered the 400 IM record to 4:06.22.

3:07, Bob said, had to be a split time, meaning an intermediate time in a given race, in this instance after the breaststroke leg, or three-quarters of the 400 IM, with only the up-and-back freestyle portion to go.

If you do that, he said, you're going to finish in 4:03-something.

That would be at least seven, nearing eight, seconds better than I had gone in first setting the record just six years before.

More than two seconds better than I had gone in Melbourne.

4:03? Obviously, some strong part of me believed I could go 4:03.

If you put a limit on anything, you put a limit on how far you can go. I don't think anything is too high. The more you use your imagination, the faster you go. If you think about doing the unthinkable, you can. The sky is the limit. That's one thing I definitely have learned from Bob: Anything is possible. I deliberately set very high goals for myself; I work very hard to get there.

4:03?

Then again, why not? No limits.

•   •   •

Every year since I have been swimming competitively, I have set goals for myself. In writing.

The goal sheet was mandatory. I got used to it and it became a habit. When I was younger, I used to scribble my goals out by hand and show the sheet to Bob. Now, I might type them on my laptop and e-mail him a copy. Each year, he would take a look at what I'd given him, or sent him, and that would be that. He wouldn't challenge me, say this one's too fast or that one's not. When I was doing this only on paper, he typically would look at it and give it back to me; now he simply files away the electronic copy I send him.

I usually kept my original paper version by the side of my bed.

The two of us are the only ones who have it, who ever got to see it.

The goal sheet was famously secret for a long time . . . Until now.

I didn't look at the sheet every day. I pretty much memorized it, how fast I wanted to swim and what I had to do to get there.

If there was a day when I was down, when I was not swimming well, when I simply felt tired or grouchy, I would look at it. It was definitely a pick-me-up.

Pretty soon after I made my first goal sheet, I hit every one of the times to a tenth of a second. Precisely. Exactly. It's like I have an innate body clock. I don't know how or why I was able to do this. I just could, and often still can. It's another way in which Bob says I'm different, and always have been.

When I was thirteen, Bob felt I needed to have some formal lessons in goal-setting. One day, on a school holiday, he surprised my mom by saying, I'm taking Michael to lunch today. He came and picked me up, and we went to this restaurant that I liked. He pulled out a sheet of paper. He said, okay, what are your goals this summer?

Of course, I replied, I don't know.

He started suggesting some things I ought to do and said, why don't we pick three events. Let's start, he said, with the 1500 meters. The 1500 is almost a mile. A Bowman favorite. We were trying, even when I was that young, to lay down a base of endurance work. Let's do that in 16 minutes flat, he said.

Let's also pick the 200 fly, Bob said, and I put down 2:04.68. That time was precisely one-hundredth of a second under the national age-group record. That would be a big drop for you, he said.

Okay.

Bob then said, let's pick the 400 IM. He suggested a time of 4:31.68, which was also near the age-group record.

He said, take this paper home and put it on your refrigerator. You'll see it every day.

That summer, at the 1999 junior nationals in Orlando, I didn't win any events.

In the 1500, I went 16:00.08. I was off by eight-hundredths of a second.

In the 400 IM, I swam 4:31.68. Precisely.

15

In the 200 fly, I swam 2:04.68. Precisely.

The 200 fly time was nearly 10 seconds better than the best time I had done in practice about six weeks beforehand, when Bob had ordered a set of three 200 flys as a tune-up.

In that 200 fly in Orlando I took third place. Bob congratulated me and said first place might have been bad luck. He said he had never coached anyone who had won juniors and then had gone on to win nationals as a senior.

Later that summer, I went to the senior nationals in Minneapolis. In my first race, I finished 41st. My next race was the 200 fly. I finished dead last in my heat, in 2:07.

This was maybe a lesson for Bob. Maybe I wasn't ready just quite yet. Maybe I was just emotionally overwhelmed. I had touched in 2:04.68 a few weeks before; logic said I should have gone at least that fast in Minneapolis.

That summer I turned fourteen. I can still remember being on the pool deck at nationals, getting ready for my heat, and thinking, there's Tom Dolan. Tom Dolan! He was 6-feet-6 and was supposed to have only 3 percent body fat. He had gone to the University of Michigan and had already won a gold medal in the 400 IM at the 1996 Summer Olympics in Atlanta. He was a legend not only for what he had done but also for how he trained: to the point of exhaustion, maybe beyond.

Another time at the meet in Minneapolis, I remember, I was sitting in the stands and there, across the pool deck, went Tom Malchow. Tom Malchow! He had gone to the University of Michigan, too. And he had won a silver medal in the 200 fly in Atlanta.

I was in awe. Here I was, on the very same pool deck with Olympic swimmers.

The last day of the meet in Minneapolis, I wasn't due to compete in any races. This meant nothing to Bob. "Get ready, Michael," he said. "You're doing a practice today."

What?

I didn't even have a suit with me. Why would I? I wasn't supposed to race.

I thought to myself, we're already at the pool, are we really going to get in the car, go back to the hotel, drive all the way back here and train?

Yes.

It took us a good 40 minutes to go there and back. I didn't like it, didn't like any of it. Bob didn't care. I went back in the water.

That fall, back in Baltimore, we started training for the 2000 spring nationals in Federal Way, Washington, near Seattle.

With six weeks to go, Bob had an idea at practice. Let's do what we did last year as a trial run: a set of three 200 flys. Into the water I went.

My best time of the three turned out to be 2:09. Bob was obviously disappointed. After the 2:04.68 from the year before, he thought I was going to do 2:05, at least. Maybe, he told me, you could even break two minutes.

In the back of his mind, Bob was holding out the possibility, no matter how remote it seemed, that I could finish in the top two at the Olympic Trials that summer in Indianapolis and make the Olympic team. At that point, I had produced nothing to suggest that the 2000 Olympics were truly possible. This did not deter Bob. He believed in me, completely.

The way swim meets work, the heats are usually in the morning or early afternoon, and the finals at night. When I was a teenager, the heats would pretty much always go off in front of just a few people in the stands, typically parents, brothers and sisters, other coaches. I have come to like a noisy crowd. Early that afternoon in Federal Way, there was almost nobody in the stands.

I went 1:59.6.

That broke the age-group record for fifteen- and sixteen-year-olds. I was still only fourteen.

That night I came back and raced the 200 fly again. I finished in 1:59.02, behind only Stephen Parry of Great Britain and Malchow.

Afterward, I had my first interview. I was asked, did you think you could break two minutes in the 200 fly? Here's what I said: My coach told me I could do it.

It's after that 1:59.6, Bob likes to say, that he knew I would make the Olympic team, maybe sooner than later. I had no idea. I was, after all, fourteen.

The day after that, I set another age-group record in the 400 IM, lowering my time in that race by seven seconds, to 4:24.

The next day, I wasn't swimming in any finals. Sightseeing? No way. Into the pool I went.

We got home from Federal Way on a school day. My mom, who was at work, had put a large banner saying, "Congratulations," on the lawn and had trimmed it in red, white, and blue. Bob, who had brought me back to the house, took down the entire display. When she got home, Mom was furious. Bob was unmoved. It was a matter, Bob said, of tempering expectations. Best to keep everything in perspective. Bob asked my mom, "What are you going to do when he wins nationals? He got third. If he wins, are you going to buy him a car? If he sets a world record, what, a house? You can't get excited about every step. There are so many steps. We're on, like, step 200 of 3,000. How are we going to keep going?"

Bob has, without question, helped refine my intense drive and dedication. He has also, without question, helped me believe that anything is possible. Two seconds faster than the world record? Doesn't matter. Three seconds faster? Doesn't matter. You can swim as fast as you want. You can do anything you want. You just have to dream it, believe it, work at it, go for it.

I wrote the sheet that lay out my goals for 2008 a few weeks after coming back from those 2007 world championships in Melbourne. That meet in Australia had been one of my best ever. I won seven gold medals and set five world records, including that 4:06.22 in the 400 IM.

In the 100 free, I wanted in the Olympic year of 2008 to go 47.50.

200 free: 1:43.5.

100 fly: 49.5.

200 fly: 1:51.1.

200 IM: 1:53.5.

And the 400 IM: 4:05 flat.

There's more on the sheet, other races as well as split times for every single race.

But these were races I was likely to swim at the Olympics.

In writing that I wanted to go 4:05 in 2008, I knew full well that was ambitious. That would be more than a full second better than I had ever done before.

And yet: 3:07.

Which meant 4:03.

• • •

I started swimming when I was seven.

Mom put me in a stroke clinic taught by one of her good friends, Cathy Lears.

"I'm cold," I remember saying.

And, "I have to go to the bathroom."

And, "Can't I just sit here and watch the other kids? I'll stay here by the side."

Mostly, I remember, I simply didn't like putting my face under the water.

Miss Cathy told me I could use the backstroke, if that's what I wanted. But I was going to check off every item on the practice plan. "You're going to learn," she said, "one way or the other."

I complained and whined some more.

Even so, I finished every item on her plan. And soon enough I learned how to flip over onto my tummy and learned to swim the freestyle.

It would be a couple years yet until I would be diagnosed with attention-deficit/hyperactivity disorder, or ADHD. All everyone knew, in particular my mom, my sisters, and my coaches, was that I had all this energy and that I could bleed off a lot of it by playing sports: baseball, soccer, lacrosse, swimming, you name it.

What I discovered soon after starting to swim was that the pool was a safe haven. I certainly couldn't have put that into words then but can look back and see it now. Two walls at either end. Lane lines on either side. A black stripe on the bottom for direction. I could go fast in the pool, it turned out, in part because being in the pool slowed down my mind.

In the water, I felt, for the first time, in control. Swimmers like to say they can "feel" the water. Even early on, I felt it. I didn't have to fight the water. Instead, I could feel how I moved in it. How to be balanced. What might make me go faster or slower.

It would be ridiculous to say that I was a world-class talent from the very start. If it wasn't for the fact that Hilary and Whitney were swimming, I probably wouldn't even have started swimming.

I was a kid. A kid who was given to whining and—it's true—crying. I was seemingly forever on the verge of tears. My coaches remember a kid who was constantly being picked on. When I was younger, it seemed like almost anything could set me off into an emotional jag or launch me into a full-on tantrum, throwing my goggles and generally carrying on.

All this agitation was probably just my way of seeking attention. Mostly, I wanted to fit in, especially with the older kids. I just wanted to be acknowledged.

And yet, amid all this drama, I already had a dream: I wanted to win an Olympic gold medal.

One.

Just one. That was it at the start. Just one medal.

I also knew that winning Olympic medals was, truly, possible. It happened to people I knew. When I was seven, Anita Nall, a North Baltimore swimmer, won a gold, a silver, and a bronze at the 1992 Olympics in Barcelona. When I was eleven, Beth Botsford, another North Baltimore swimmer, won two gold medals in Atlanta.

My Olympic ambitions might not have been obvious, granted, especially early on and especially in the mornings, when I'd have to get up for practice. I have never been what you'd call enthusiastic about being up early in the morning.

Mom would come to get me out of bed. It would still be dark out. She would turn on a soft light in my room, a little night-light, and say, "Good morning, Michael. It's time for morning workout."

I would grump and groan.

Mom would go down the steps. I would just lie there in bed, nice and comfy. A few minutes later, she would come back and say, "Pop-Tarts are coming out of the toaster now. I'll be in the car waiting for you. Pick them up on your way out the door, because Bob's expecting you at workout."

My mom would go out to the car and sit, waiting for me. Bob is a morning person. He likes to get up before dawn. It's his favorite part of the day. Always has been.

Later, into middle school and high school, I remember driving in the dark to the pool and there never being any lights on at any house on the way there, and it would just be my mom and me, alone, going to practice. Sometimes my mom would yawn; I still can't believe how loud she sounds when she is yawning.

Once my mom had dropped me off at Meadowbrook, about 15 minutes away from where we lived, in Towson, Maryland, I usually wouldn't make it home again until it was dark again. Bob would take me from practice to school, or to breakfast and then to school, and then in the afternoon we would go back to the pool. Mom would come get me at maybe seven at night.

I would always be the last one out of the pool. She was always working so late; I remember it seemed like I was always the last one to leave. Unless I'd been kicked out of practice early by Bob, for not doing what he wanted the way he wanted it done or when he wanted it done; in that case, I had to sit there and wait for her, anyway.

All of this driving around, the back and forth on the roads around her job, required enormous dedication and sacrifice on my mom's part. At the same time, it was a total reflection of who she is. And that's something I am forever grateful for.

She made it abundantly clear that we—she, my sisters, me— came first, even as she insisted that we have a passion for life itself and for something, or some variety of things.

We had to have goals, drive, and determination. We would work for whatever we were going to get. We were going to strive for excellence, and to reach excellence you have to work at it and for it.

Mom calls this common sense. She grew up in a blue-collar area of western Maryland. Her father was a carpenter. Her mother's father was a miner. Neither of my mom's parents went to college. They had four children—Mom was the second of the four—and all four are college graduates; Mom went on to earn a master's degree.

My dad, Fred, used to take me fishing when I was a little boy. He would take me to Baltimore Orioles games. He taught me to look people in the eye when I was meeting them and to shake hands like I meant it. He was a good athlete himself—a small-college football player—and, unquestionably, I inherited my competitive athletic drive from him. If I was playing sports, no matter what it was, my father's direction was simple: Go hard and, remember, good guys finish second. That didn't mean that you were supposed to be a jerk, but it did mean that you were there to compete as hard as you could. The time to be friends was after the race; during it, the idea was to win.

My mother and father were high-school sweethearts in a mill

town in western Maryland. Dad played football at Fairmont (West Virginia) State College; Mom followed him there. After they were married, they moved to the Baltimore area. My father moved out of the house when I was seven. As time went on, we spent less and less time together. Eventually, I stopped trying to include him in my activities and he, in turn, stopped trying to involve himself in mine.

The last time I saw my father was at Whitney's wedding, in October 2005. He and I didn't talk at the wedding; there just hasn't been anything to say for a while. Maybe there will be later.

Having said that, I feel I have everything and everyone that anyone could ever ask for. I have the greatest people in the world around me and supporting me.

My mom is an educator, now a school principal, and her passion in life is changing the lives of children. When she recognized a passion in her children for swimming, she was all in to help each of us.

At the same time, things were going to be done in our house, and done a certain way, because that's the way it was. Homework was going to get done. Clothes were going to get picked up off the floor. Kids were going to get taken to practice. We were all in it together.

Not only that: Our house was always the home where any kid was welcome. If there was a kid who needed to stay over to make swim practice the next morning, we had a sleeping bag and a pillow.

That work ethic, and that sense of teamwork, was always in our home. All of that went to the pool with me, from a very early age.

It's why, when I won my first Olympic gold medal, the first people I wanted to see when I had a quiet moment were my mom and my sisters.

• • •

They say that what the decathlon is to track and field, the 400 individual medley is to swimming.

Most swimmers, like the vast majority of those who compete in track and field, are specialists. They do the backstroke, for instance. Or the breaststroke. That's not to say they don't know how to swim the other strokes. They do. But once they get to a certain age, they usually compete only in the one they're best in.

That's why the IM is tough. You have to do all four strokes, and do them all well.

The 400 IM is tougher still because it's all four strokes and at distance. It requires strength, endurance, technique, and versatility.

This race can make you hurt bad. Your shoulders start to burn. Your legs ache. You can't get a breath. The pain is sometimes dull, throbbing. It's like your body isn't even in the unbelievably great shape it's in. All you want is for the pain to stop.

Who's the mentally toughest? That's what the 400 IM is all about.

I had won the 400 IM at the 2003 championships in Barcelona in what was then a world-record time, 4:09.09.

A year later, as I got ready to get into the pool for the 400 IM Olympic final in Athens, Rowdy Gaines, himself an Olympic champion in 1984, now an NBC analyst, was saying that this was the race that was going introduce America to Michael Phelps.

I knew well the recent Olympic history of the event: Americans had gone 1–2 in the 400 IM in 1996 and in 2000. Dolan had won in Atlanta in 1996; Eric Namesnik, another Michigan man, had gotten silver. In 2000, Dolan repeated as Olympic champion; Erik Vendt, who had grown up in Massachusetts and gone to the University of Southern California, took silver.

Lining up that Saturday evening in Athens, I was in Lane 4, Vendt in Lane 1.

I have since watched the video of this race dozens of times, maybe hundreds. It's the one race that, from the eight days of competition in Athens, still stands out most to me.

After the butterfly leg, I led by more than a second; after the back, more than three, more than two body lengths ahead. The breaststroke had long been the weakest of my strokes. It was imperative on this leg that I not give up ground. I didn't.

100 meters to go. I turned and started doing the free.

50.

The swimmers who swim the fastest in the heats are assigned in the finals to the middle lanes. The advantage of swimming in the middle is that it's easier to keep an eye on what everyone else is doing. Coming off the last wall, I saw that Alessio Boggiatto of Italy in Lane 3 was still approaching his turn; in Lane 5, Hungary's Laszlo Cseh was not yet at the wall, either.

I still had that one lap to go.

But I knew already that I had won.

And so, underwater, I smiled.

Not even a half-minute later, I glided into the wall, and I was still smiling.

I popped up and looked for Mom in the stands. Even before I looked at the scoreboard, I looked for Mom, and, there she was, standing next to Whitney and Hilary, all of them cheering and just going crazy. I turned to look at the clock. It said, "WR," meaning world record, next to my name. 4:08.26. I raised my arm into the air.

I had done it.

I had won the Olympic gold medal I had been dreaming of since I was little.

I had also, in that instant, become the first American gold medalist of the 2004 Athens Games.

I really didn't know what to do, or say, or think.

"Mike! Mike!"

It was Vendt. He was swimming over from Lane 1. Truthfully,

in the excitement of the moment, I hadn't noticed yet that he had finished second. We had gone 1–2. Cseh had finished third.

In finishing second, Vendt had carried on one of the quirkiest streaks in Olympic history. Four Games in a row an American named Erik or Eric had finished second in the 400 IM; Namesnik had taken silver in 1992 as well.

"Yeah, Vendt! Yeah!" I shouted. "Yeah! We did it!"

I could not stop smiling.

"So proud of you," Bob said.

"It felt great," I replied.

A little while later the top three finishers were called to the medals stand. An olive wreath went onto my head, the gold medal around my neck. The American flag went up, along with another for Vendt's silver and the Hungarian flag for Cseh's bronze. The "Star-Spangled Banner" began to play. I took the wreath off my head. The right thing to do is to take a hat off your head for the anthem; maybe a wreath was the same.

As I listened to the anthem, playing for me, for my country, my eyes grew moist. Even so, I could not stop smiling.

I had done it.

After warming down, I grabbed my cell phone.

When Mom and my sisters go to meets, Hilary is the keeper of the phone.

"Where are you guys?" I asked her.

"We're over by a fence, behind you. They're going to kick us out."

"Hold on. I want to see you guys. Meet at the gate."

Bob went with me, along with a doping official who was doing his official thing, just keeping an eye on me as he was supposed to do. Nothing untoward, nothing unusual about it. I walked toward the fence, my gold medal around my neck. My mom didn't see Bob or the doping guy. She just saw me. To my mom it looked like I was ten, back at Meadowbrook. I had my

gold medal around my neck and, in her mind's eye, a peanut butter and jelly sandwich in my hand.

I put the medal through the fence and said, "Look, Mom.
Look what I did."

•   •   •

That 400 IM in Athens was, as I see it, the turning point. I was
nineteen. I had my first Olympic gold. My mom and sisters were
there to watch—that was, to me, what meant so much.

I did not go on to win eight gold medals in Athens. I won six.
Eight overall, six gold, two bronze.

On the one hand, the Athens Olympics were an extraordinary
success for me. I had met the original goal and gone well beyond.

On the other, I did not meet all my expectations.

Thus I had ample motivation to keep swimming, keep pushing myself. Beijing was four years away. That's a long time. And
yet not.

Because stuff happens.

In the fall of 2004, I had major worries about my back.

A year later, I broke a bone in my hand.

In 2008, two years after that, I broke my wrist.

So many newspaper, magazine, and website stories have been
written about me that sometimes it seems almost everything
about me has been well documented.

But not everything.

I was so worried about my back in 2004: It turned out I had a
small stress fracture, and needed rest. There were times I would be
in Bob's office feeling broken down physically and emotionally.
Whitney had endured back problems that seriously affected her
career. I was scared and worried. Plenty scared, seriously worried.

I can't emphasize enough how, during all this, Bob was there
for me. This is the side of him that doesn't get depicted often in all
the stories that have been written about us, which tend to focus on

how it's his way or the highway; this was the side that reminded me why I would never swim for any other coach. Bob made it plain how much he cared. He stayed positive. He sought, time and again, to reassure me. He would say, you're fine, we're going to get through this, we're going to get your back taken care of, it's all going to work out. Which, ultimately, it did.

Later, in the fall of 2005, the first week of November, I was hanging out in Ann Arbor with a bunch of swimmers. I was not in a very good state of mind. I don't remember why. Boys will be boys, I guess.

In fact, I don't recall very much about the entire thing except that we were at this guy's house and I hit something with my right hand—maybe a post, maybe a wall. I don't even remember why I hit it. I'm not aggressive like that. It was just a weird situation. To this day, I have no idea why I did it. But it happened.

The bone underneath the pinky on my right hand broke in half. It popped, just like that. The bone almost came out of the skin.

I put my left hand over it and tried to hold it in place.

I called Keenan Robinson, a trainer at the University of Michigan I had come to trust and rely upon, and he helped me put it in a temporary splint, then got me to the emergency room.

Keenan called Bob. Bob called me back a bunch of times on my phone. I didn't answer. Bob called a girl I was seeing at the time, trying to get her to answer. It wasn't until the next night that he finally got me on my cell.

It was not a pleasant call. I have bad news, I said. Oh, God, he said. After that he said, we really need to get our act together, "we" meaning me. I know what I did was stupid, I said. I know I made a mistake. I can't change it.

Ultimately, I underwent surgery. Doctors fixed the break with a titanium plate and three screws. Keenan did an amazing job helping me with the therapy; the scar is hardly noticeable.

Bob was amazed at how quickly I was able to come back. I

rode the stationary bike hard until I was allowed back in the water; the day after Thanksgiving I was back at it.

Fall and early winter are typically not big months on the swimming calendar and while obviously a certain number of people in Ann Arbor knew about the break, Bob and I didn't advertise it.

My second broken bone is far better known.

Then again, the time pressure the second time around was very different.

In the fall of 2007, after dinner one night at Buffalo Wild Wings in Ann Arbor, one of those restaurants with a sports theme, I was walking to my car. As I neared it, walking on the driver's side, I slipped. I fell down and hit the ground. In reacting— you don't really have time to think in this kind of situation—I put my right hand down to cushion the fall. I caught myself. Nothing hurt. Everything seemed all right.

The next morning, Sunday, I woke up and it looked like there was a golf ball on my right wrist.

I thought, this isn't good.

This can't be good.

This could be really bad.

No way I was calling Bob. At least not first.

I called Keenan and said, "Can you come over and look at something?"

He replied, "What is it?"

This was, after all, Sunday morning. It's not like anyone would have been anxious to roll right over.

"It's like there's this giant golf ball on my wrist. I slipped last night and fell."

A few minutes later, Keenan showed up. As soon as he started touching the wrist, started trying to manipulate it, I felt nauseous. Literally sick to my stomach. It was the same feeling I had when he had touched the hand two years before.

I knew right then the wrist was cracked. Fractured. Broken.

I started doing some quick math in my head.

This was late October. The Games were the next August. Two full months left in 2007 plus seven months in 2008. Would there be time?

Wait. The Trials were at the end of June. Two months in 2007, plus less than six months in 2008 to get ready. Would there be time?

I was not sure. I worried that I might be done, not just for the Olympics, but for my entire swim career. I was a mess. In tears.

Keenan said, we have to call Bob.

Bob had decided that day that he was going to make soup. He had gone to Whole Foods and stocked up on vegetables. He was going to make himself a huge pot of sumptuous vegetable soup.

Keenan called Bob. Bob told Keenan, put Michael on the phone.

I was as upset as I could be. I told Bob, I think I just gave away gold medals. I guess it was a good try, I said. I'd had a good run. I don't know how I'm going to be able to come back from this.

Bob listened quietly.

He said, the meet's not next week. Let's see what you can do. He also said, I was there for you in the beginning; I'm going to be here at the end, and however it ends up is how it ends up.

After we hung up, I found out later, Bob threw out his soup. He suddenly had no appetite.

Keenan took me to the emergency room. X-rays confirmed it was broken. At the hospital, I was asked for my autograph; I'm right-handed and couldn't sign. So I was asked for photos. While hooked up to IV lines.

The next day, Keenan, Bob, and I went to see the surgeon. One of the things about being at the University of Michigan, which after the incident two years before I knew full well, is that they have there some of the greatest doctors and nurses in the world. The surgeon said we had two options:

Let it heal on its own, which would take a while. That's what most people do, the doctor said. Your hand would be in a cast for maybe six weeks, he said.

I said, what's the other choice?

Surgery, he said, the advantage of which would be that the bone would be put back into place then and there with a pin, and you'd simply wait for the stitches to come out. About ten days, he said.

That was a no-brainer.

Surgery it was. "You're talking only one pin?" Bob said, mindful that the prior break had involved three screws and a plate.

I said, "When's the next available date?"

They couldn't schedule the surgery immediately; it would be a few days away.

Meanwhile, Bob heard, "Ten days," and thought, okay, maybe this isn't the end of the world. What my clumsiness had done, he made clear, was eliminate my margins. Before the break, I maybe had some wiggle room in my schedule. Now I would have none.

"You can still do this," Bob told me. "But are you ready to listen?"

"Yes."

"Starting right now," he said, "you're going to have to do every single thing I ask you to do. You're going to have to do it my way."

I thought to myself, this is not going to be fun. But that's not what I said.

"Okay," I said. "I'll do it."

I finally worked up the courage to call Mom and tell her, too. That is, I called during school hours, when I knew she would be working and wouldn't have her cell phone with her, and got voice mail. Mom, I said, I've had this little incident on the curb; it's okay, Keenan's taking care of me; talk to you later.

When Mom heard that, she said later, she thought, Oh, good God.

We had gone to the doctor in the morning. That afternoon, per Bob's instructions, I was on a stationary bike.

For me, riding a stationary bike is one of the most boring activities imaginable. It's horrible. One of the worst things I've ever done. Some people think swimming is boring or monotonous. Not me; swimming is fun. Riding a stationary bike is the least amount of fun possible. The thing was, though, I knew I needed to keep working out. The bike was making my legs stronger. Much as I didn't want to do it, I did it. It was the right thing to do. I had given Bob my word. I was going to do exactly what he wanted, exactly how he wanted it done. I rode that bike every day until I underwent the surgery. Bob gave me a day, maybe two, and then I was back on the bike. A few days after that, I had my hand in a plastic bag, and I was back in the water, kicking.

In a weird way, the broken wrist gave me an urgency that in the long run turned out to be a positive.

Right after Thanksgiving, at the short-course national championships in Atlanta—short course in the United States usually means the races are held in a 25-yard pool—I dove in against Ryan Lochte in the 200-yard individual medley. Ryan set an American record, 1:40.08; I finished second in 1:41.32, Eric Shanteau came in third at 1:44.12. Bob couldn't have been more pleased. Here I had not even had the chance to swim even 50 yards of butterfly since the break and yet I could step it up against Ryan, maybe the best short-course racer in the world.

I remember going to a meet in Long Beach, California, in early January, and being asked there about the broken wrist. The scar on my wrist was still fresh, still purple.

The accident, I said, had made me refocus on 2008, which was going to be the biggest year of my life, and my goals.

I told a pack of reporters who were there, "If I could live in a bubble right now, I probably would, so I couldn't get hurt, I couldn't get in trouble, I couldn't do anything. Just swim, eat, and sleep. That's it."

I also said, "I think I'm more excited now than when that happened." I added, "I plan on not screwing around anymore until after the Olympics. I have pretty hefty goals this year. It's going to take a lot to get there."

•　　•　　•

To get there meant placing first or second in my individual races at the Olympic Trials.

The Trials are never a formality.

It didn't matter that I had won eight medals in Athens. That was then. The fact that I had won the 400 IM at the 2004 Olympics would have absolutely no bearing on whether I would, for instance, again enjoy the privilege of representing the United States at the 2008 Games in the same event. I had to earn it.

Different countries allocate spots on their Olympic teams in different ways. Some, for instance, do it based on results over the preceding years; some allow coaches to pick; some pick by committee.

That's not the American way, at least in swimming. There are no picks.

In the United States, there's only one way to make the Olympic swim team in the individual events: first or second in that race at the Trials.

Third gets you a four-year wait to try again. If you can.

Hayley McGregory finished third in the 2004 Trials in both the 100 and 200 backstrokes. She would go on at the 2008 Trials to set a world record in the 100 back in the preliminaries; in the finals, she finished third. In the 200 back, she finished third. She did not make the team.

It can be like that. So cruel.

"If I'm third at the Olympics, it means I'm on the medal stand in a few minutes. If I'm third at the Trials, it means I'm on the couch for a month," Gary Hall, Jr., one of the most accomplished American sprinters of the last twenty years, once said. Winner of ten Olympic medals between 1996 and 2004, twice the gold medalist in the 50-meter sprint, Gary would finish fourth in the 50 in Omaha. He did not make the 2008 team.

Our selection process is without question the most difficult in the world, far more nerve-wracking than the Olympics, actually, because the depth in the United States in swimming is unmatched anywhere in the world.

And the 2008 Trials were going to be the deepest in history.

During the same week the swim Trials were going on in Omaha, the U.S. Trials in track and field took place in Eugene, Oregon. All over Eugene—at the airport, on buses, on highway billboards—advertisements declared the U.S. track team the "hardest team to make."

Wrong. It's the swim team.

In track, the top three in each event to go the Games.

In swimming, only two.

It figured that, in the 400 IM, those two would be me and Lochte. But nobody was handing us anything. And Lochte was hardly ready to concede first place to me.

A couple months before the Trials, the U.S. Olympic Committee holds what's called a media summit. It gathers a bunch of athletes it figures are good candidates to make the Olympic team and, for the better part of a week, allows hundreds of reporters to have a crack at asking questions for the features their editors want before the Olympics start. Then the athletes can go back to training without being pestered by reporters for the duration.

The 2008 media summit took place in Chicago, at one of the city's landmark hotels, the Palmer House Hilton. At the summit, Lochte was asked about racing me. "I always feel like I can beat him," he said.

Lochte is a good friend, one of my best friends in swimming. It's one of those deals where we are hardly alike but like a lot of the same stuff. I call him Doggy. No good reason. Doggy is a Florida surfer dude; I grew up near Baltimore. Doggy's idol is the rapper Lil Wayne, who is also one of my favorite musicians. Doggy sometimes wears gold chains around his neck, baggy pants, a diamond-encrusted grill in his mouth. Cool that it's Lochte's style; not mine. I have a bulldog named Herman. Lochte's dog, a Doberman, is named Carter, after Lil Wayne, whose real name is Dwayne Michael Carter, Jr. In May, Lochte sprained his left ankle when Carter the dog ran out the front door of Lochte's house in Gainesville; chasing Carter down the street, Lochte said he turned the ankle. At least that was one version of the story. His dad later said it happened after a skateboarding trick gone bad. Who knows? Doggy is a free spirit.

A free spirit who is a hellacious competitor.

Lochte had won silver in the 200 IM in Athens. He didn't swim the 400 IM in Athens because he had finished fourth at the 2004 Trials, 10 seconds behind me. At the 2006 U.S. nationals, Lochte had narrowed the gap to about a second and a half. At the 2007 worlds in Melbourne, I had beaten him again, this time by about three seconds.

I had not lost a major-meet final in the 400 IM since I started swimming it at the national level. Even so, I knew what I was up against: maybe the second-best all-around swimmer in the world.

I also knew, though, that I had improved, even since Melbourne, even taking into account the broken wrist. My breaststroke had very quietly gotten way better than it had been. In practice, I had been working on subtle differences: keeping my shoulders closer to my ears, my hands flatter, my fingertips up when I accelerated forward. At that Long Beach meet in January, a short-course event, I raced the 100-yard breaststroke; the field included Mark Gangloff, who had come in fourth in the 100-meter breast final in Athens. Mark won the race that night, in

53.09 seconds and, for most, the reporters and the people in the stands, that seemed to be the news—that I'd lost. To me and Bob, that was not at all the news. Instead, to us, it was that I'd finished just behind Mark, in 53.41. I had almost beaten one of the world's best breaststrokers, only a few weeks after surgery. Bob said later, that was one of the most impressive things he'd ever seen me do.

At the same time, my backstroke, for some reason, had been giving me fits. I didn't have the consistency I wanted. And my 400 IM times through the early months of 2008 had been unremarkable. At a meet in Santa Clara, California, six weeks before the Trials, I won the 400 IM in a flat 4:13.47. My backstroke felt horrible that night, as it had for the previous few weeks. I had no tempo. My kick wasn't there. Instead of 100 meters, I felt like I was swimming a mile on my back. However, two days later, still in Santa Clara, I beat Aaron Peirsol in the 100-meter backstroke. Aaron had won the 100 back in Athens. This was the first time I had ever beaten him in a backstroke event.

So maybe the backstroke was there, after all. I really couldn't be sure.

At some meets, the 400 IM is last on the agenda; that's the way it was in Barcelona, at the 2003 Worlds.

In Beijing, as in Athens, it would be first.

So, in Omaha, at a temporary pool in the middle of the Qwest Center, the best set-up for a meet in the history of American swimming, it would be first, too, as USA Swimming deliberately set up the program for the Trials to mirror the schedule in Beijing.

My first swim in Omaha, the prelims of the 400 IM, turned out not good. I finished in 4:13.43. Lochte, swimming in a different heat, was timed in 4:13.38, faster by five-hundredths of a second.

Lochte told reporters afterward that his ankle was, in fact, bothering him: "The hardest part was the dive. As soon as I dived in, it was like, ugh."

I told reporters, "I'm not really too happy."

In fact, I had gone to meet Bob and told him, I feel awful.

A few minutes later, I had definitive proof. I did feel awful. My lactate test said so.

When you do anything physical, like swimming, and particularly if you're swimming all-out, that exertion creates lactic acid. In scientific circles, there is controversy over whether lactic acid itself is the thing that drags down athletic performance or whether other stuff within the body, signaled by elevated levels of lactic acid, causes fatigue. It doesn't matter to us swimmers. What matters is that we are constantly tested to see the rate at which we can clear lactate from our systems because that indicates our ability to recover.

That's why, at most top meets, moments after a race you can see a parade of swimmers lining up for individual lactate tests. Someone pricks your ear and collects a few drops of blood; those drops are then placed into a machine, which measures the number of millimoles of lactate per liter of blood. For me, the point is to drop the level as close to 2 as possible. The way to make it drop is to swim easily for a certain number of minutes.

These swims are held in a separate pool just steps away from the competition pool. Ideally, you're taking the lactate test three minutes after leaving the competition pool, and then it's into the warm-down pool. The lactate test tells me how long I then need to swim down; typically, it's between 17 and 22 minutes.

My lactate reading after the prelim 400 IM swim read 12.3.

Superhigh.

Nerves, I guess. I had no other explanation. I remember feeling momentarily flustered. Why was my lactate so high? I had a long swim-down to think about it.

At that point, I just wanted to get onto the team. If I was going to have a loss, I started rationalizing, if only for an instant, better at the Trials than at the Olympics.

As soon as I thought that, though, I also thought this: One thing I am for sure good at is responding. At the risk of being obvious, I have an enormous appetite for competition, and a huge will to win. Always have.

Eddie Reese, who is the swim coach at the University of Texas, and also had the honor of being the U.S. men's swim coach at the 2004 and 2008 Olympics, has a saying: 80 percent of swimmers like to win, 20 percent hate to lose, and 95 percent of the Olympic team comes from the hate-to-lose group. When I'm focused, there is not one single thing, person, anything that can stand in my way of doing something. There is not. If I want something bad enough, I feel I'm gonna get there. That's just how I've always been.

So to make the team—no, to win the 400 IM at these Trials—I had to refocus, and quickly. In the finals that night, I had to get a lead. If I did that, I felt confident my competitive instinct would come out. No matter how tired I was, how painful it was, I would get there first, would hold Lochte off.

But it was going to be a battle.

The prelims took place at eleven that Sunday morning Central time; the finals went off at seven that evening.

Just before the finals, my racing gear already on, I went to my bag and took two salt tablets. Bob looked at me quizzically.

He said nothing.

I said nothing.

If I had told him how I was truly feeling, he would have freaked.

My heart was racing. Like an out-of-control freight train barreling down a set of tracks, that kind of racing.

This had been a problem for me dating back at least eight years, to the first time I'd had one of these episodes. Then it was at a practice. My heart rate elevated and, for what seemed an eternity, wouldn't come down. Ultimately, the pounding subsided and we didn't think anything of it until it happened again. Then we went for a battery of tests, including for Marfan syndrome, a disease that affects connective tissues and can be fatal if there is leaking in the vessels that lead to the heart. Flo Hyman, one of the best volleyball players of all time, a silver medalist at the 1984 Los Angeles Summer Games, who died suddenly during a match, had Marfan, though nobody knew that until an autopsy revealed the disorder.

As it turned out, I did not have Marfan. Instead, the doctors said, I was a salty sweater, meaning, simply, I lost high amounts of salt in my sweat. When I got below a certain sodium level, I got dehydrated easily.

The easy fix to this was to supplement my diet with salt pills.

For all the years since I first went to the doctors about this, Bob's concern—make that his out-and-out fear—had been that I would have one of these incidents at a meet.

And here it was happening in Omaha, just moments before the first race of the Trials was to be broadcast live on NBC.

I knew that if I'd told Bob, it might have sent him over the edge. Just imagine: Live from Omaha! Here he is, Michael Phelps! And he's clutching his chest!

Which is why I didn't say anything.

I just had to go out there and swim.

Once that first swim is over, if it's good, I have momentum. Then the meet feels as if it's all going downhill. It's just getting past that first swim. Four years of work, dedication, drive, and commitment all distilled into four minutes of racing. This was going to be the gateway, the first race in answering what I was going to be doing in Beijing, and how I was likely to do it.

In track they have a starter's pistol that signals the start of a race. In swimming it's a beep.

Beep!

After the opening butterfly leg, I had a lead of about a body length on Lochte.

In the back, he closed to half a length.

In the breast, he pulled even.

With 50 meters to go, the question was clear: Who had enough left?

As I turned, I glanced over at Lochte. I saw where he was. As Lochte rose to the surface, I was still underwater, surging, dolphin-kicking. When I finally broke the surface—the rules are 15 meters underwater, no more—I had left Lochte behind.

I touched in 4:05.25. A new world record.

Lochte finished in 4:06.08. Both of us had gone under the prior record, my 4:06.22. And he was supposed to have a banged-up ankle that was bothering him?

The two of us were far, far ahead of the rest of the field. Robert Margalis, who finished third, was more than seven seconds behind Ryan, eight behind me.

"Nice job, Doggy," I said to him after it was over.

"That hurt," he said.

"Yeah, tell me about it," I said. Then I told him, "We got this in Beijing. Let's go for it. Let's go get gold and silver in Beijing."

All smiles, I saw Bob a few moments later. That's when I let him in on how my heart had been galloping along beforehand. I didn't tell you because I knew it would turn you catatonic, I said.

Lochte's time that night was three seconds better than he had ever gone before. At this level, that's an incredible amount of time to knock off. If I was planning on me getting gold in the 400 IM in Beijing, Lochte silver—for sure, Lochte obviously had other plans. But the question Lochte would now have swirling around inside his head was: Could he get better still, or had he already maxed out?

"Going into the race, I thought I could beat him. I hate to lose. I don't like it at all," Lochte said afterward.

He also said—and this is why after the Trials, heading toward Beijing, I thought the 400 IM could be the toughest individual race on my schedule—"I know there are a lot of places where I can improve."

• • •

Though I respect Lochte immensely, love to race him, understand—I was not afraid of him, concerned about him, worried about him.

Whatever he was doing to get himself ready for the Olympics was out of my control.

I don't worry about other guys when I'm training, not even Lochte. I get myself ready. Of course I'm racing at the Olympics, or anywhere, against other guys. But I'm also racing against the clock. And, maybe mostly, against myself, to see how good I can be.

That said, I want to be clear: I have the utmost respect for my competitors. I love to race them. Those guys help me. The faster they get, the faster I get, because I don't want to lose.

If I could do 4:05 at Trials, I thought, maybe I really could do 4:03. My lactate response after the 4:05 proved perfectly normal. Which made me think: I'd had a racing heartbeat beforehand yet had thrown down a world record, and immediately afterward the blood work showed I was completely back to normal.

Which made me also think that it's all in how you respond to pressure.

I also knew there were things I could fix to get me to 4:03. I knew my breaststroke could be faster. I knew I could go out harder in the fly and still be relaxed. That's one of the biggest things I have in the medley; I can go out so much faster than other guys in the fly, that first leg, yet be more relaxed and comfortable. It's called easy speed. I have it.

3:07.

The dream kept visiting me throughout my week in Omaha, as I went on to qualify to represent the United States at the Beijing Games in five individual events: the 400 IM, 200 free, 200 fly, 200 IM, and 100 fly.

I also swam 47.92 in the preliminaries of the 100 free, the

tenth-fastest time ever. The point of that swim was to be in the pool for the 400 free relay, nothing more. I didn't even swim the semifinals or finals of the 100 free.

After the Trials, then, it seemed all but certain I would swim at the Games in three relays: the 400 free, the 800 free, and the 400 medley.

All in, eight chances for gold.

All in, including preliminary and semifinal swims, 17 races in just nine days.

After the Trials, all of us on the U.S. team went off to Palo Alto, California, for a training camp; then to Singapore, for more practice but in the same time zone as Beijing; then, finally, on to Beijing.

In Palo Alto, I was on my game. Bob said it felt like every day in Palo Alto for him, watching me, was like Christmas. However, Lochte was on, too.

Lochte and I don't do a lot of head-to-head sets because, as Bob figures, somebody's likely to learn something about the other guy. One morning, however, we lined up for a complicated set, four of each stroke, that ended with fast 50s of each stroke—fast meaning race pace. On the fly, Lochte was close to me; on the back, dead even; on the breast, he was perhaps a full second ahead, a huge difference; we were dead even again on the free.

I was happy with the set. Bob was happy, too, but you could almost see him thinking, hmmm. I knew he had noticed how fast Lochte had gone during the breast.

If I never once imagined Ryan beating me, Bob probably thought about it every day. Maybe that's the way we have to go.

The Singapore camp was mostly about resting and recovering, not hard training. I did do one butterfly set that undeniably hinted at what kind of shape I was in: three 100 flys, with easy 200s in between, each 100 faster than the other. I did the last one in 51.6. It was maybe the best practice I had ever done, and just to put it in perspective: A week before the 2007 Worlds in

Melbourne, I pushed a 53.8, which Bob and I both thought was terrific.

So, a 51.6. Bob walked over to another one of the American coaches and said with a big smile, well, my work is done, I'm officially on vacation.

Hardly. But we were both feeling good about where I was.

When swimmers are gearing up for a big meet, we go through a cycle that's called "shave and taper." As the meet draws near, the idea is to keep training but include more rest, drawing on the weeks and months of hard training beforehand, the objective being to peak at the meet itself. That's called the taper. The challenge is in getting the timing right, complicated by the fact that what works for one swimmer might not—indeed probably won't—work for another. There's no one-size-fits-all. Bob puts it this way: When you taper swimmers, it's like a haircut. You never know if it's any good until it's too late.

That 51.6 also suggested my taper was dead-on where it needed to be.

As for the shave, swimmers shave their bodies before a major competition on the theory that body hair creates resistance. You have to shave everywhere; well, everywhere that isn't covered by your suit. It makes you feel clean and smooth. Super-clean and super-smooth.

For most of the winter, in Ann Arbor, I had let my beard grow. As the year went on, I showed up at most pre-Olympic events with facial hair, sometimes a goatee, other times an excellent Fu Manchu. I'm just messing around with it a little bit, I told everyone after we got to Beijing, sporting the Fu.

When the facial hair goes away, that's how you know I'm getting serious.

I showed up for my first Olympic swim in Beijing, the prelims of the 400 IM, clean shaven. Even the hair on the back of my neck was neatly trimmed. Courtesy of Lochte.

He didn't have me trim his; he likes to keep his hair long and shaggy. Besides, no one would trust me with clippers. Or at least no one should.

If it seems just a little weird that Lochte would be trimming my hair one day and then we'd be racing each other two days after that for Olympic gold—well, that's both the way swimming is and the way he and I get along. Someone's got to trim the hair on the back of your neck if you want it done, right?

During one of the media scrums before the Olympics started, Lochte had said, "When me and Michael talk, it's strictly anything but swimming. We don't talk about swimming at all. That's—I guess that's good for both of us. We're not always getting wound up in this whole Olympic thing. I mean, we have down time to relax."

The day before the 400 medley prelims, Friday, August 8, was the day of the opening ceremony. Much as I would have loved to have gone to the ceremony, there was just no way; I had to swim the next day and couldn't run the risk of marching and then standing in the heat and humidity.

I didn't want to get up and worry about shaving the morning of the prelims, which were the following night, so I decided to shave down then. In our little suite in the Olympic Village, there was nothing on the floor to keep the water from the shower inside the shower itself; we were forever, it seemed, dealing with a small flood. I was in the shower, with my music on, shaving, and Lochte yelled out, hey, why are you shaving now?

When I explained to him what was up, he decided he would shave then, too.

While we were in the midst of shaving down, I said, referring to the 400 IM, let's finish this. One-two again. Erik and I did it in Athens. Dolan and Erik did it in Sydney. Dolan and Namesnik in Atlanta.

Let's get after it, I said.

Let's get after it, he said.

I knew I had to have a good first race, and that was a very

good thing. I can't emphasize it enough: A good first race sets the tone.

Laszlo Cseh, the Hungarian who had won the bronze in Athens, was in the first of the three seeded heats. He went 4:09.26. I watched that and thought, I'm going to have to go faster if I want to be in the middle lane in the final. And I definitely wanted to be in the middle in this race.

Lochte went in the next heat. 4:10.33. At this point, with my heat still to go, five guys had already gone 4:12 or better. I was thinking, okay, get after it.

At 150 meters, my butterfly leg already over, halfway through the backstroke, I realized I was going fast. I was, in fact, under world-record pace. I thought to myself, not so fast, not tonight. The last 200 meters, I put it on cruise control. I hit the wall, took my goggles off, looked at the clock, and saw 4:07.82.

An Olympic record.

I did not expect that at all.

My prelim time was a full 44-hundredths better than my winning time in the finals in Athens.

And honestly, while this prelim race didn't hurt that bad, my strokes didn't feel the way I quite wanted them to. I could do better.

Cseh was asked after the prelims if he could win. "That will be hard," he told the reporter. "I'll try everything but that will be hard. If somebody wants to win this race, they need a 4:05." His personal best, as I knew well, was 4:07.96.

Lochte said, "If I'm right there with him, then there's pressure. We'll see what happens."

I felt no pressure. My plan was to get some sleep and be ready to go in the morning.

Amid dreams of 3:07.

• • •

In the summer of 2001, Jacques Rogge, who at that time was the newly elected president of the International Olympic Committee, had a conversation with Dick Ebersol, the chairman of NBC Sports. NBC, as it had since 1988, would be broadcasting the Summer Games. Beijing is twelve hours ahead of New York. The 2000 Olympics from Sydney, fifteen hours ahead of New York, had largely been shown on tape delay. That had rubbed some critics entirely the wrong way. Now, Ebersol wanted to know, was it possible for certain events in Beijing—swimming and gymnastics, mostly—to be moved around, switched so the finals took place in the morning, Beijing time? If so, they could be shown live in prime time on the East Coast on NBC, which was paying the IOC nearly $900 million for the right to broadcast the Beijing Olympics.

Rogge said he'd have to get back to Ebersol. The IOC president would have to check with the heads of the international swimming and gymnastics federations. At an Olympics, even though most people think the IOC is in charge of everything, those federations are actually still in charge of running the sports themselves.

More than three years later, Rogge got back to Ebersol. Yes, he said, swimming and gymnastics would be moved.

Over Thanksgiving weekend in 2004, Dick Ebersol was seriously injured in a plane crash in Telluride, Colorado; his son, Charlie, survived the crash; a younger son, Teddy, was killed. Several months later, on what turned out to be the very first day that Dick returned to work, my mom and I happened to be in New York. We asked if we could drop by his office; we wanted to see how Dick and his family were doing. With us was Drew Johnson, who, working with Peter Carlisle, is part of my team at Octagon, the agency that represents me.

It was a very, very emotional meeting.

Sitting in his office, Dick said at one point, I have something to tell you. I want your reaction, please understand it's going to happen no matter what you say, but I want you to know: the swim finals are going to go off in the morning, the heats at night. Would that be a problem?

No way.

I was thrilled.

For real.

Swimming being on during prime time is everything I want for the sport, I told him. I'm trying to leave the sport bigger and better than it was when I was lucky enough to have first found it.

Dick asked me not to tell anyone about the news until it broke, which it eventually did, of course, after which I was asked repeatedly what I thought about swimming in morning finals.

It's the Olympics, I responded. If you can't get up to swim in the morning, don't go.

Which I believed 100 percent. Swimmers swim in the morning, anyway. To get to the Olympics and represent your country is an enormous privilege. How could anyone seriously think about not being able to perform? To say that you didn't want to give your best because it was ten in the morning instead of eight at night was an excuse.

The Olympics are no place for excuses.

The morning of the 400 IM final, Sunday, August 10, I met Bob at our dorm in the village—he was on the first floor, I was on the third—for a wake-up swim at a pool in the village. I was maybe ten minutes late meeting him. That sort of thing drives Bob crazy, especially on race day. He kept looking at his watch but not saying anything. Just looking at the watch.

We had never done a wake-up swim before. Some coaches swear by them. Not Bob. But we'd never had a morning final before, and Bob didn't want to spend the next thirty years wondering if he should have had me do a wake-up swim. So I did 500 to 800 meters, just enough to get moving.

Lochte had already done his wake-up swim. Katie Hoff, who is from Baltimore, too, and is an old friend, was doing hers. She would go on to win three medals in Beijing.

After that, we walked over to the dining hall for breakfast: oatmeal and fruit. And one of those cultural moments: no brown sugar for the oatmeal. I used white sugar. No excuses.

By now we were only three or four minutes behind Bob's schedule. He kept looking at the watch.

This was his way of saying, I want to get this first race over and done with.

Me, too.

For years, I've had the same routine to get ready for a race. I got to the Cube, per the routine, two hours before the race.

Like I always do, I stretched and loosened up a bit first. Then I got into the water, wearing just a brief; it's not the time for competition-style suits, much less full-body gear, and swam my warm-up: 800 mixer to start, alternating a 50 freestyle with a 50 of something else, anything but free; 600 meters of kicking with a kickboard; 400 meters of pulling a pull buoy; however I want to do it, something to warm up my arms; a 200 medley drill; then some 25s just to get the heart going a little bit. Since I was getting ready for a 400 medley, I also did one or two 25s of each stroke. When I was done with that, I swam down for 75 to 100 meters.

That was that.

Usually, while I'm doing this warm-up, Bob goes and gets himself a Diet Coke or a coffee—straight-up black, of course. Not this day. We were both feeling slightly paranoid. I asked him to stick around at one end of the pool with my water bottle. That way we could make extra certain no one was going to do anything outlandishly stupid like trying to poison me.

Warm-up went by uneventfully. I dried off, got warm, put my headphones on, and sat on the massage table. I always sit; I don't lie down. From that point on, no matter the event, Bob and I don't talk until after the end of the race. I mean, what's there to say?

In Beijing, the headphones were plugged into a black iPod, which I had gotten as a bonus for buying an Apple laptop at a store in Ann Arbor a few months before the Olympics. Here was the deal at the store: iPod or free printer. I never print anything so I grabbed the iPod. What's on my iPod? Lil Wayne and Young Jeezy, to name two, especially Young Jeezy's "Go Getta" and Lil Wayne's "I'm Me." The lyrics to "I'm Me" are definitely not G-rated. But that's not, for me, the point. When I hear Lil Wayne do that song, I hear him saying, I'm my own individual, and that's me.

At the Cube, there was a television in front of the massage table. The choices invariably seemed to be archery, volleyball, or women's basketball.

About forty-five minutes out, I hopped into my suit, the Speedo LZR Racer. Some guys like to wear a brief under the LZR. Not my way. Under the LZR it's me. Some swimmers have said they need help putting on the LZR. Not me. I put a plastic garbage bag on my foot and rolled that leg of the suit over the bag, then up my leg; then I put the bag on the other foot and did it on that side. Easy.

For the individual medley I wore a suit that went from waist to the ankles—essentially swim pants. It can feel too constricting, especially trying to do the butterfly, to wear a full suit, one that wraps over the collarbones.

With thirty minutes to go, I got into the water again to do 600 to 800 meters. I was in the water for ten minutes, max. I got out, dried off, and grabbed my USA parka, put my warm-up pants on, put the headphones back on.

With about ten minutes to go, I grabbed my credential and walked to the ready room. The credential is your ID pass at the Olympics; it's a laminated plastic card that includes a picture and a barcode. For security reasons, you can't go anywhere without it.

When I'm in the ready room, I'm there by myself and to be by myself. Usually, the officials who are in the room try to sit all the guys in the same row if you're in the same race or the same heat. I never do that. I just find a seat where I can sit by myself and block the two seats on either side; my caps and goggles go on one, towel on the other.

Lochte came over and said, good luck. I was, like, thanks, man, let's do it.

I knew, and Lochte knew that I knew, that, unfortunately, he wasn't quite himself. He had been dealing with a pretty significant case of the runs. It appeared McDonald's was his attempted solution. For a few days, he had been eating religiously at the one in the village cafeteria, chowing down each time on what seemed to be more than a dozen Chicken McNuggets, a burger or two, and fries. Lunch and dinner. If Lochte wasn't quite himself that day, well, he'd had an ankle problem at the Trials and went under the world record. He was going to bring it as hard as he could, no question.

They called our race. I put on the goggles and caps.

It was time to go.

As I walked out onto the deck, I looked for President Bush; I'd heard he was in the audience. I found him after a few moments, and it looked like he was pointing at me, waving his flag.

After we walked out to behind the blocks, I did what I always do there. I stretched my legs on the blocks, two different stretches, one a straight-leg stretch, the other with a bent knee, left leg first.

I took the right headphone out.

Once they called my name, I took the left headphone out, the parka off. It's my routine to stand on the left side of the block and get onto it from that side.

I made sure the block itself was dry. This is a lesson learned the hard way. At the 2004 Santa Clara meet, before the 400 IM, I didn't notice the block was wet. Instead of diving in, I more or less fell off the block. Embarrassing. Since then I've always made sure to wipe the block with a towel.

Once up there, like I always do, I swung my arms, flapped them, really, in front and then in back, slapping my back.

Some people have suggested that's a routine I do to psych people out. They think that I'm thinking: Even if you can't see me well behind your goggles, here's the sound that's announcing you're going to get your butt kicked. Nothing of the sort. That would be poor sportsmanship in the extreme. It's just a routine. My routine. It's the routine I've gone through my whole life. I'm not going to change it.

I get asked all the time what I think about when I'm up on the blocks, in the instant before the starter says, take your marks.

Nothing.

There's nothing I can change, nothing I can do to get faster. I've done all the training. All I can do is listen for the beep, dive in the water, and swim.

•   •   •

I had told Bob I intended this 400 IM to be the last one I would ever swim competitively.

It's not that I couldn't swim it again. More, I simply didn't want to. It's that demanding.

If I was going to go out, then I wanted to go out in style.

The idea in the first 50 was to use that easy speed and then turn it on just enough so that at 100 I would have a lead of half a body length, maybe even a full body.

At the first wall, Cseh was in first. I was just behind. Perfect.

The next 50, I gave it a little more juice. As the fly leg ended, I was in first, Cseh second, Lochte third.

I figured I'd be ahead after the next 100 as well, after the backstroke.

Lochte apparently had a different idea.

He went out hard over the first 50 of the back and turned there in first.

At 200, I was back in front but not as far ahead as I had planned when I was visualizing. Lochte was just behind me, Cseh third.

We turned for the breaststroke.

This was where Lochte apparently thought he could school me. No way.

The breaststroke felt as good as my breaststroke has ever felt.

Coming off that 300 wall, I had no idea where either Lochte or Cseh was. I knew only that I had to give it everything I had in the free.

It wasn't until I turned at 350 that I knew what was what. I was in Lane 4. Cseh was in Lane 5, the one next over to my right; Lochte in 6, one more over. When I came off the 350 wall and took my first breath, turning my head to the right to breathe, which was in their direction, I couldn't see either of them, couldn't see the splash from their hands. I was way ahead, and suddenly I had the same feeling I had in Athens. You take your first freestyle stroke on that last leg, the race is almost over, and you're in the lead. Underwater, just as I'd done four years before, I smiled. I smiled as I churned for home, going strong.

After touching, I whipped around so fast, trying to see my time on the big scoreboard at the other end of the Cube, that I bumped my head into the wall.

The scoreboard said I had hammered home in 4:03.84.

Just as I had dreamed it.

My 300 split time: 3:07.05.

4:03.84. I had smashed my own world record by 1.41 seconds. Even I had to say to myself, *wow*.

A little more deliberately now, I leaned up against the wall, then onto the lane line and raised my arms above my head, touchdown style.

Bob was nodding his head up and down in approval, a big smile on his face.

In the stands across the way, my mom gave Whitney a kiss,

then put her hands over her face in relief and almost disbelief. Hilary wiped away tears.

Back the other way again, President Bush and the First Lady, and their daughter Barbara, along with the president's father, President George H. W. Bush, were waving and cheering. President Bush gave me a point and a head nod. Cool. I said thanks with a big smile. Later, he told me, "God, what a thrill to cheer for you!"

Wow.

Looking at the scoreboard, I could see that Cseh had finished second, more than two seconds behind me, in 4:06.16. Lochte had gone out too hard in the first leg of the backstroke and paid for it at the end of the race. He was third, more than four seconds back, in 4:08.09.

"I saw Lochte going (slower) and I tried to do everything to go better than Phelps, but I don't have too much power for that," Cseh said. "Anytime you think you can get close to Michael Phelps, he jumps to another level."

I got out and met Bob. That was awesome, he said. Let's swim down.

Later, looking at the numbers closely, Bob said this might have been my best race.

Not like my best race of the year. He meant the best race I had ever done. Considering the circumstances, taking into account all the pressure and distractions and the buildup and the general noise around me and the Games; it was exceptional, he said.

On two of the four legs, I swam faster on the second length than the first. On the backstroke, for instance: 31.37 going out, 30.2 coming home. On freestyle: 28.94 going out, 27.85 coming back.

There's a term in swimming for going faster in the back length than the first. It's called "negative splitting," and it's a strategy that certainly doesn't work for most everyone else. Common sense says it ought to be harder to go faster on the back half than the front.

It's just the way I've always done it.

Where I really won the race, what made me happiest, was that I had dominated in breaststroke. All the practice, the focus, the effort on the breast had paid off. Cseh was more than three-tenths of a second slower over that 100 meters; Lochte's breast leg was more than a second behind mine.

I had ripped through the first 50 in the breast in 34.77. That was a lifetime best. I came back in 35.79. Not a negative split but still, it got me to 300 right at 3:07.

Wow.

On and around the pool deck, my world-record time instantaneously generated an enormous buzz. I had become the only man in history to have broken the world record in winning both my Olympic 400 IM golds.

Eddie Reese, our U.S. men's head coach, told reporters, "We just don't know how good that is. If somebody ten or fifteen years ago would have said the 400 IM will be won in 2008 in 4:03.8, I'd have bet everything I had or would ever get that it wouldn't happen."

As soon as Bob finished telling me the swim was awesome, he reverted to coach mode. He actually had visualized himself how he would coach at this exact moment, not getting overly excited over any one race.

Even though, as we talked about later, he was also thinking to himself that it may really be hard for Michael to get beat.

On the medals stand a little while after the race, the American flags, along with the Hungarian one, went up, just like in Athens. But no wreath this time.

As the flags were lifted up into the rafters, as "The Star-Spangled Banner" played, my eyes started watering. For me, this was a rare public show of emotion. I couldn't help it, didn't want to help it. I was thinking of all the ups and downs I had weathered since Athens, how hard I had worked, the sacrifices that had been made by so many to help get me to just this moment.

I so appreciated all of it.

I thought to myself: Sing. Sing out the national anthem there on the podium. But I couldn't stop crying.

Bob got teary-eyed, too, glad there was no camera on him.

Just when it looked like I might start sobbing or something, as the anthem reached ". . . the home of the brave," the music accidentally cut off.

All I could do was laugh.

And think: seven more chances, maybe, for the Chinese to get the American anthem right.

2

BELIEF:
THE 400 FREE RELAY

Bob is not the most technologically advanced individual. He has, however, discovered a little something on the Internet called Google. This was, for him, a major advance. Now he could read almost anything and everything written about me, and us, and about swimming in general.

I don't bother reading much, if any, of it. It can seem overwhelming.

Bob is not overwhelmed. He loves fishing for stories. And he not only reads but remembers what was said.

I won the 400 IM on Sunday morning, the 10th. Because the schedule was flipped—finals in the morning, prelims and heats often at night—the Sunday night schedule included the heats of the 400 free relay. I didn't swim in those heats; instead, I raced in the prelims of the 200 freestyle.

At major swim meets such as the Olympics, the guys who swim the prelims for the American team are not the same four guys who swim the final. There are good reasons for that. One, the prelim saves the guys in the finals lineup from the exertion of an added race. And, two, the prelims give more guys a chance to make the Olympic team, with the bonus that if the finals guys win a medal, the prelim swimmers get that medal, too. So, for instance, a winning swim in the finals means a gold medal not just for those four guys but for each of the prelim swimmers, too. It works the same way in track and field. The prelim guys get a medal if the finals guys do.

At the U.S. Olympic Trials, the prospect of being on the relays makes the 100 and 200 freestyle races that much more exciting. The top two finishers earn the right to swim in the individual event at the Games as well as the relay; for example, the 100 winner gets to swim in the 100 at the Games and the 400 relay. But the third- through sixth-place guys get to go to the Olympics, too, at the very least for the relay prelims, in some cases, the relay final.

Garrett had won the 100 at the Trials. Jason had come in second.

Cullen finished third.

Then came Nathan Adrian, Matt Grevers, and Ben Wildman-Tobriner.

For the finals, Garrett and Jason were locks, and so was I, because of the 47.92 I had produced at the Trials.

Cullen, Nathan, Matt, and Ben would be swimming the prelims with extra incentive. The one who swam the fastest split in the prelims would get to swim in the finals, too.

Each of them was fully deserving.

Cullen is, in a family sense, somewhat like me. He's very close to his mother. In his case, his dad died of lung cancer when Cullen was sixteen; his mother is invariably at our meets and you can tell that he has a very, very good relationship with her. Cullen was born in New York City and nearly drowned as a child when the inner tube he was riding at a water park flipped over. He didn't know how to swim. It took CPR, oxygen, paramedics, all of it to save his life. After that, his parents put him in swim class. In 2006, at the Pan Pacific Swimming Championships, one of the major meets of that year, he set a meet record in winning the 50 free. Cullen, Jason, Neil Walker, and I won the 400 free relay and set a world record, which made Cullen the first African-American swimmer to hold or share a long-course record. Making the Beijing team meant he was the third African-American to make the U.S. Olympic swim team, after Anthony Ervin and Maritza Correia. Cullen was a big part of a USA Swimming program called "Make a Splash," which is based on chilling statistics: Nearly six of every ten black Americans can't swim and African-American kids ages five to fourteen are nearly three times as likely to die of drowning as their white counterparts. One of the reasons that's cited for the dismal figures on minority swimmers—Hispanic-Americans are also far more likely to drown at a young age—is a lack of role models. His message is obvious, so simple, so common-sense: Hey, black kids can swim, too.

Nathan, who's from Washington state and took off what would have been his sophomore year at Berkeley to train for the Olympics, is one of those guys who's poised to be in the next great wave of top American swimmers. He was nineteen in the summer of 2008. "I think Nathan Adrian is a phenomenal talent and you can expect great things from him," Gary Hall, Jr., with whom Nathan had been training, said at the Trials. Mark Schubert, the USA Swimming head coach, said that Nathan "reminds me of Matt Biondi in 1984," which is high praise, no doubt. Matt, who also went to Cal, won five gold medals at the Olympics in 1988 in Seoul. Nathan's story was great because it's not just that he finished fourth in the 100 at the Trials; it's how he got there. In the semifinals, he had finished in 48.89. That was good enough only for a tie in ninth place, with Alex Righi. Only the top eight go on to the finals. Then, though, Lochte scratched from the 100 final to concentrate on other events, the 200 back and the 200 IM. So

Nathan and Alex had a swim-off. Just the two of them in the pool. Nathan won. That got him to the finals and then, in the finals, swimming in an outside lane, he got that fourth-place finish.

Of all the guys on the American team, Matt is the one Bob had been watching with particular interest. Both of Matt's parents are Dutch; thus, he could have swum for Holland. He said, nope, I'm an American. President Bush liked that story so much he told it, with Matt among those looking on, at a ceremony in the Rose Garden in July, before the Olympics. Matt grew up in Lake Forest, Illinois, north of Chicago, and swam in college for Northwestern, where he was a four-time NCAA champion and earned twenty-seven All-America citations. As good as he was there, he got even better when he moved after graduating in 2007 to Tucson, Arizona, to train with Frank Busch and Rick DeMont.

Ben, like Matt, is a phenomenally smart guy. He was a Rhodes Scholar finalist in the fall of 2007, after graduating from Stanford with a degree in biomechanical engineering, and was bound for medical school after the Olympics. His grandfather was a justice on the California Supreme Court. All this, and Ben had won the 50 free at the 2007 Worlds in Melbourne.

When Nathan, Cullen, Ben, and Matt lined up in that order on the blocks on Sunday night in the first of the two relay heats, the world-record still stood at 3:12.46, the time that Cullen and I had helped set in 2006 at the Pan Pacs.

So much for that. When Matt, swimming the anchor leg, touched, the scoreboard said, 3:12.23.

In that heat, the Australians finished second, in 3:12.41, under the 2006 mark, too.

In the next heat, the French finished in 3:12.36, again under what had been the record time.

Afterward, one of the French swimmers, Frederick Bousquet, said, "I talked to my coach, and he said the ideal position was to finish second behind the United States, and they beat the world record and they come in as favorites tomorrow, and tomorrow morning we take all that they have."

He also said he had looked at the four Americans in the ready room just before the prelims and saw uncertainty. "They didn't look at us, although they usually do," he said. "We could sense that they were a little bit afraid."

These remarks followed those of another French swimmer, Alain Bernard, who at the European championships in March had set a world record in the 100 free: 47.5, same as my goal time for 2008. Amid his arrival in Beijing, he uncorked some trash talking.

"The Americans? We're going to smash them. That's what we came here for.

"I'll start my Games in the 4x100 meters freestyle relay final, confident that my pals will have qualified easily.

"If the relay goes according to plans, then we'll be on a roll."

The next morning, Monday the 11th, Bob and I were at the village dining hall, along with Jason and maybe one or two others. Bob, the Internet sleuth, had found the French comments. He said, hey, guess what I read, then proceeded to describe what he had found.

Bob added, and here came a loaded code phrase that he knew would carry extra zing, it says here they think they're pretty much going to smash you like guitars.

Comments like that just make me more fired up.

I said, that's nice; this is going to be fun.

•　　•　　•

There's no point in talking smack, absolutely no need to talk beforehand about what you're going to do. It's not worth it, not worth playing the mind games. Just get in the water and swim. People who talk about what they're going to do, nine times out of ten don't back it up. It's always better, and a whole lot smarter, not to say anything, to simply let the swimming do the talking.

There's a saying that goes precisely to the point, of course: Actions speak louder than words.

That saying is 100 percent true.

That saying is one of Bob Bowman's all-time favorites.

I learned that early on.

Every summer, the North Baltimore club holds a long-course meet. It's one of the major events on the NBAC calendar. The night before the meet—this was when I was maybe twelve, not all that long after Bob and I had started working together—he was overseeing what was, for him, a pretty easy practice. At the end of it, he asked our group to swim four 50s. Give me a little effort, he said. Well, of all the kids in the group, there was only one who was not giving Bob that little effort. One of the girls in the group even said, Michael, you'd better get going or we're going to have to do this all over.

Everybody got out of the pool, and Bob said, okay, everybody, that'll be it, except, and now he looked right at me, for you.

I uncorked one of the great twelve-year-old tantrums of all time. I screamed, you can't make me do it! And so on. A huge, horrible, public scene, a direct challenge to Bob's authority in front of everyone.

Bob said to me, you can do what you want, but as of now you're not a member of NBAC, and until you come back and do the set, you never will be.

I went home in tears.

That night, Mom called Bob. He told her, until Michael does the set he can't be in the meet. So what, she said, can we do?

Take a meeting, that's what. At five-thirty the next morning.

The meeting was in the club's aerobics room. Bob had set up a table and four chairs.

Four?

I showed up with a baseball hat on my head. Bob made me take it off. Mom and I sat down on two of the chairs, Bob grabbed a third. And in came my father, a Maryland state trooper, in full uniform. My eyes got wide. At that point, my father was still much more involved in my life; even so, for him to show up like that, at that hour of the morning, meant this was no-doubt-about-it serious.

Bob said, Michael, there's a triangle here. There's your dad. Your mom. Me. Guess who's in the middle?

Me, I said, very softly.

That's right, he said. You've got nowhere to run, nowhere to hide. You have to do what we want you to do.

Bob turned to my parents. Before Michael can swim in the meet, Bob said, he has to do the set.

So I did.

And I had to do it to Bob's satisfaction.

Which I did.

When Bob and I started, he knew of me mostly as Whitney's younger brother. He had been introduced as North Baltimore's new assistant the day after I turned eleven. One day, our team was swimming at Towson State, and two of the kids started throwing towels and soap around the men's bathroom. I walked in; some of the older kids started shouting out my name, as if I'd been the one who started the whole thing. In walked Bob.

"Michael Phelps," he said, "what did you do?"

"I didn't do anything! It was them!"

"Well, then why are they shouting your name?"

"Ask them."

"No, Michael. I'm asking you. What did you do?"

Nothing, at least that day. As I walked out there, I thought, it'll really stink if I ever have to work with that guy. As Bob walked away, he was thinking, thank goodness I will never have to coach that kid.

That's how it all began. I thought he was a such a jerk. I thought, no way I'm ever swimming for him.

He soon realized I was just scared out of my mind.

A few months later, the North Baltimore club executed a staff shake-up. Bob was put in charge of a set of promising swimmers ranging in age from high school to me.

I still remember the first set he gave us: a 400 free, a 400 stroke of any sort, one 400 IM and a 400 free. I did each set three times. I still remember it because it hurt. A lot.

Mostly, Bob wanted to see how we would react.

He watched me finish the final set of four 100 frees with intrigue. I was coming back faster at the end of set—1:05 for each hundred—than at the beginning. He didn't know then what to make of that.

Another early set went like this: a 200 freestyle to start; then a 200 IM; four 50s of each stroke; four 100 frees with a small break in between each one—what's called an interval, the time between depending on any number of things—ending with a 400 IM. We were asked to do this particular set four times. I was twelve, and I just killed it, had a great set. Maybe, Bob thought, this kid really could be something special.

A few months after Bob had been coaching me, he issued orders for a pretty difficult practice, especially for someone my age. When it was over, all the other kids were dragging. They got out of the pool slowly. They got their towels and clothes slowly. I got out but still had a ton of energy, so much that I kept running to the side of the pool, filling up my cap with water and dumping the water on the other kids' heads. Bob ran over to tell me to knock it off. He told me that if I was still this frisky he could for sure make practices a lot harder.

I said, and Bob has never forgotten this, I will never get tired.

We have since dispelled that rumor.

You have to be mentally tough to go through it with Bob. If you're not mentally tough, you're not learning what he's teaching you. Growing up, I used to tell Bob when he would order a set that would make my eyes widen, I can't do that. He would say, there's a difference between "can't" and "won't." Maybe you won't do that, he would then say. But you can.

If you say "can't," you're restricting what you can do or ever will do. You can use your imagination to do whatever you want. "Can't," he would say, that's a tough word.

Early on, Bob put me through a butterfly workout that went on for 3,000 meters. That was nearly two miles of only butterfly.

When things started getting much more serious, in my mid-teens, I was worked through a freestyle set that went on for 12,000 meters. That's about seven miles. It went like this: one 800, two 700s, three 600s, four 500s, five 400s, six 300s, seven 200s, eight 100s.

I would do a set built on this combination: 300 free, 200 fly. Each 500 amounted to one. I did ten.

The worst sets ever would involve long repetitions, say thirty 100s, bad enough, but with a twist. At the 50-meter mark you'd have to climb out of the pool, then start the remaining 50 from the blocks. One of my favorite sets, Bob likes to say, because getting out of the pool and diving back in adds an extra component to the thing that's just brutal. After twenty, you're grabbing the block. You can't see straight. Things are blurry. You feel like you can't move.

But you can. That's what I came to understand. At that point it's pretty much just goals. If you want to meet your goals, this is what it takes.

●   ●   ●

Bob was born and raised in South Carolina. He was an accomplished musician and artist and president of his high school's National Honor Society. He was also a swimmer. Unlike everything else he did, swimming didn't come quite so easily. Even so, he got to Florida State on a swim scholarship and, training with the distance swimmers, qualified for the 1985 spring nationals in the 100 fly. He should have been training with the sprinters, but figured more work meant better.

Not always.

Finishing up at Florida State, Bob got a job coaching with a local swim club. His boss gave him a stack of stuff to read with the understanding Bob was supposed to get it read in a month. He read it all that night, came back the next morning and asked for more.

Early in his coaching career, Bob was perhaps even more impatient and demanding. In nine years, he coached in seven places in five states.

One of those stops came in Napa Valley, north of San Francisco. There he learned from Paul Bergen. In 2001, Inge de Bruijn of the Netherlands won three individual events at a world championships; Tracy Caulkins had done it before her, in 1978. Paul Bergen coached both of them.

Paul was exacting. So is Bob.

Paul liked to train thoroughbred horses. Bob, too. Plus: Horses don't talk. Swimmers can't, either, at least when swimming. Bob and I would learn to communicate without saying a word.

Bob didn't come to Baltimore with the slightest intention of coaching me. He had been turned down in 1995 for what he thought then was his dream job, head coach of the Dynamo Swim Club in Atlanta. The club offered the job to someone else. Bob thought, that's it. He decided to try for a degree in farm management at Auburn University, thinking he ultimately would run a horse farm. While he was there, he figured, he would take a part-time assistant's job at Auburn.

The 1996 Olympics in Atlanta were coming up. Looking for advice, he spoke with Murray Stephens, the head coach at North Baltimore. Murray had trained Anita Nall and Beth Botsford. Murray had developed a culture that demanded excellence. He respected Bob.

How much, Murray asked, is the Auburn job paying?

Told $10,000, Murray said, we'll pay you $35,000. When can you start?

Bob said, how about next week?

From that very first day, even if he hardly showed it, Bob knew I was, as he likes to say now, made for swimming.

My growth spurt came before I turned fifteen. By that time, I was almost as tall as I am now. Getting that big that fast obviously increased the length of my stroke. That meant I could do more in the water and thus became way more accepting of Bob's ever-increasing demands. In turn, he could tell, as could I, that I kept getting better and better.

Which gave me genuine confidence.

Another slogan Bob likes is one from Bill Parcells, the football coach: You can't dream up confidence. Confidence is born of demonstrated ability.

Even when he saw me at eleven, saw my body, the way I was built, Bob knew I would be an excellent swimmer.

I was blessed with very large hands and feet. My feet are now size fourteen. My hands have been compared to dinner plates. Big hands and feet are one of the things coaches look for; they're tools that give a swimmer an excellent way to hold onto the water while swimming. The very best swimmers carry very few bubbles, very little air, when you look at their hands and feet under water; they're able to slide their hands in, and to position both hands and feet on the water, where they're the most effective. That's what "holding onto the water" means.

I have a long torso in relation to my legs. That helps me plane on top of the water like, well, a boat.

My wingspan is longer than my height. I'm now 6-foot-4. My wingspan is three inches longer, 6-foot-7. A swimmer with long arms who takes longer strokes obviously ought to be able to take fewer strokes in a single lap; that can be a big advantage.

In a way, I'm both perfectly tall and short. My shoulders are wide but my waist is only 32 inches. I have the torso of someone 6-foot-8 but the legs of someone more like 6 feet exactly. In the water, that means lower drag.

I'm very flexible in my shoulders, elbows, knees, and ankles. That's big in swimming because what you want to be able to do is to exert a lot of force but do so fluidly. Also, flexibility gives you a range of motion by which you can hold the water more effectively. The flexibility in my ankles means I can whip my feet through the water as if they were fins.

Flexibility runs in the family. Whitney, when she was a competitive swimmer, used to be able to lock hands behind her back and bring them up, without unlocking, over her shoulders, all the way in front.

Also, I have a very high endurance capacity. Some of this is because I started swimming at seven and had, by the time Bob arrived at NBAC, put in four years in the pool. That was truly important in developing my heart and lung capacity. They think now that you can really do a lot with a young athlete, before he or she hits puberty, to build endurance for later on; longer swimming sets when you're young, for example. That's exactly what I did.

At ages nine and ten, I was swimming seventy-five minutes per day four times a week, then ninety minutes per day five times a week.

At age eleven and twelve, I moved up to swimming every day of the week, each time for two and one-half hours.

With all of that, what struck Bob the most about me when we first started together was not anything physical.

It was what was in my head.

Then as now, I was intensely competitive. Not just in the pool. In anything.

Who was going to be first into the front seat of the car?

Who was going to pick out the first video at Blockbuster?

Who was going to be first at the dinner table?

In practice, I always tried to lap as many people as I could. But I was never, in my head, training against them because I never, ever trained against other people. I always trained against the clock.

At meets, I always wanted to win. I absolutely hated to lose.

Nothing about that has ever changed.

With Bob's prompting, I discovered something else about myself early on, too. I could be motivated not just by winning. By improving my strokes. Hitting split times. Setting records. Doing my best times. There were any number of things I could do to get better. Winning never gets old, but there was a way to win that showed I was getting better, and could get better still.

Bob used to say to me, let's just see what you've got in you; use all the gas in the tank. I started using his saying. I would say to him before a meet, let's just see what I have in me. I wouldn't say, I want to win. It would be, I want to see what I have in me.

At the same time, Bob emphasized sportsmanship, accountability, responsibility. The program placed an extraordinary premium on attitude. It was said, over and again, that the single most important factor in anything we do, and particularly in this endeavor, was this: What is your attitude?

At NBAC, one of the slogans, and Bob had a million slogans, was, "Attitude, Action, Achievement." That was the order in which you could expect things to happen. You could see every day's practice as an ordeal. Or you could see it as adventure.

To that end, Bob would always tell me when I was younger: We become what we think about most.

Bob also used to give a talk that went something like this: Are you going to wait until after you win your gold medal to have a good attitude? No. You're going to do it beforehand. You have to have the right mental attitude, and go from there. You're going to be an Olympic champion in attitude long before there's a gold medal around your neck.

The thing that got me the most, and still does, was to take swimming away from me. NBAC had a program for perfect attendance at practice; if you made each practice, you got to wear a yellow cap that said, in blue letters, "100% Never Settle For Less." I was always wearing a yellow cap.

Bob is one of the most passionate people I've ever seen at what he does. Ever. He works around the clock. I really feel that he lives for the sport of swimming. He is up and going at it way before the sun peeks into the sky. He gets to the pool two hours before I'm out of bed. I've never seen anybody who does what he does. And he brought me along from a kid who really couldn't swim any strokes the way they're supposed to be done to where I am today.

Bob began to remake my strokes the summer I was twelve. Of course he knew exactly what he was doing; he had come to the NBAC with numerous American Swim Coaches Association awards for teaching stroke technique, and his first job was to reshape my basic two-beat freestyle kick to the more advanced six-beat kick.

He pushed. I pushed right back.

On purpose, I would lapse into the basic kick, what I knew and what I also knew had worked for me until then. Other times I'd just be lazy and do two beats. Either way, Bob would kick me out of practice, yellow cap and all. When I'd call my mom, she would tell me, no, she could not leave work early to come get me. I would have to wait until practice was supposed to be over. That's when she would come get me.

This went on until I started doing what I was supposed to do. The first day I went through an entire day of using a six-beat kick is the day Bob out-and-out dared me. He told me I wasn't old enough or mature enough to do it.

I did it.

If it sounds now like Bob was a trainer breaking the wild horse that was me, well, it is what it is.

It was much the same with morning practices, meaning a move to two practices a day, morning and afternoon. All first-rate swimmers practice both morning and afternoon. For months, I resisted. I relented after some college kids told me, hey, you know you might really get a lot better and a lot faster if you get in the pool in the morning, too. Or maybe Bob simply wore me down.

A few months after I turned twelve, Bob had called for a meeting with my mom and my father. It took place at Meadowbrook, upstairs in the babysitting room.

It was possible, Bob said, that Michael might one day make the Olympics. I'm not saying he will. I'm saying he could.

Come on, Bob, my mom said. She was in education. She saw kids every day. Michael's just a kid, she said. We don't know how he's going to change when the hormones kick in. When he wants to hang with other kids in high school.

That's why we're talking now, Bob said. Michael could be the real deal. I don't know when, he said, but he could if everyone here is willing to make the commitment.

And, he added, if he truly, genuinely loves it.

Bob talked about where they might send me to high school, what the schedule of a typical day might look like, and what sorts of sacrifices I would make, that we would all have to make. For one, he said, Michael ought to stop playing other sports. This was big. His concern was not just the time that other sports were taking away from practice in the pool, it was that I'd get hurt playing something else. Because I was so energetic, I would bounce from sport to sport to sport. I was the kid with a stick in his hand, a glove, a ball, whatever. One particular afternoon when I was nine stretched into evening, then into night, all of it around sports: I went first to a lacrosse game, where I told the coach I could only play the first three quarters; then to the baseball field, where I'd been selected for a home-run derby; then to the pool for practice until after it got dark outside.

Bob said, we're going to take this sort of thing and ease back. He also told my parents, this has to be normal. Don't talk about anything that you don't normally talk about. We're just going to enjoy the sport of swimming. And then we're going to see where it takes us.

• • •

There were, of course, choices that had to be made.

My academic track in high school had to be designed, with help from teachers and school administrators, to allow me to fulfill the essential Maryland state requirements for a diploma but no more. No honors classes, no advanced placement. Could it be worked out so that I might on some days be allowed to arrive at school later than the other kids? Might it be possible to be let out early?

Homework got done. In my mother's house, homework always got done.

There was, naturally, push-back from some in the school. A teacher once said to my mom, I taught your son very little chemistry. She replied that, during that school year, my son visited five countries because of swimming. Which was going to be more important in his life? Seeing what life was like in those five countries, or knowing how many atoms there are in so many grams of carbon-12?

There were other sorts of sacrifice as well.

My freshman year in high school, I wanted to fit in with my football-playing friends.

Let's talk about this, Michael, my mom said.

How many hours of practice a week would you have to commit to in order to play football? Where is football likely to take your friends? Will they make the varsity team? As high school goes along, will they make the county championships? Area all-star teams? Are any of them likely to be good enough to get a Division I scholarship? Play in the pros?

I doubt any of them are going to play in the NFL, I said.

Okay, she said. Now, what can you do with swimming?

I did not play football.

We went through much the same drill when I made a play to be on the school's golf team; it was a noncontact sport, I pointed out. Another nonstarter.

Mom calls what she did "planting seeds." One winter day when I was in high school, it snowed. I suddenly wanted to go sledding. Mom said, oh, are you going to go to the world championships this summer or are you going to break your arm now?

Maybe, I said after I had a second to think, I shouldn't go sledding.

That's a good idea, she said. Because you're the one who'd be calling Bob to tell him you broke your arm, not me.

This was all about learning to weigh options and make decisions. Mom might have asked leading questions to help me get to the smarter choice. But I had to make the decision myself: Did I love swimming enough to push myself to be the very best I could be?

My goals in swimming were set particularly high because they were not—were never—limited to just one stroke. I wanted to do multiple events. I wanted to try everything. Bob simply reinforced that when he made me redo my strokes.

As we went along, Bob's biggest challenge became keeping a step ahead of me. I quickly picked up a keen understanding of how his program operates and how it is put together. To keep it fresh he had to find ways to change it up. He knew that would not only provide variety; it would keep me focused.

So, for instance, I would be asked to swim with my arms only, or my legs only, or with one arm or one leg.

I would even do butterfly and backstroke legs using only my right or left arm. That would isolate the one arm and make me concentrate on the way it moved through the water.

To improve my freestyle technique, I would do a drill that involved me keeping my elbows high while I pulled through the water with my fingertips. That would make my legs do more of the work.

I would swim in sneakers. While tethered to a pulley. Wearing a scuba vest. With an inner tube around my ankles.

All of these devices worked to increase resistance, the same way a baseball player takes swings in the warm-up circle with a donut on the bat. When the donut comes off, and it's time get in the batter's box for real, that bat feels a whole lot lighter and easier to swing.

A week before Bob and I would leave for Federal Way, Washington, those 2000 spring nationals where I would swim 1:59.02 in the 200 fly, Bob convened another meeting. This time it was with my mom, outside Meadowbrook.

"When we get back from Seattle," Bob said, "we should talk."

"Why, Bob? What's wrong?"

"Nothing is wrong at all. In fact, it's all good. But it's a matter of time before things start to change for Michael and nothing is going to be the same."

"What do you mean?"

"He's way ahead of schedule right now and, at some point, I don't know when, we're going to need to get ready for media attention, hype, expectations. He'll need to prepare for that, and it will be on us sooner than we think."

By then, Bob had for weeks been feverishly trying to assess possibilities for 2000, and the Sydney Olympics. He figured that I was suddenly in the mix for Sydney. Come 2004, I ought to make the team and probably win medals, maybe multiple medals. And in 2008, who knew? There were so many uncertainties, so many unforeseeable twists and turns along any journey. But come 2008 I might do something staggering. Something no one had ever done before.

●   ●   ●

A few weeks after the swim in Federal Way, I went to a meet at the University of Michigan. There I made the Trials qualifying standard in all of the events I entered. Jon Urbanchek, the Michigan coach, had first seen me swim when I was eleven; his daughter was living in Baltimore and so he had stopped by. Urbanchek had been keeping an eye on me since—the boy might be a promising college swimmer—and said at that meet that I would probably make the 2000 Olympic team even though very few people knew even the first thing about me.

That June, as I turned fifteen, I held the American age-group records for boys ages thirteen to fourteen in both the 200 and 400 individual medleys, the 100 and 200 butterflys, and the 400 and 800 freestyles.

Swim geeks knew about me, maybe.

They also knew that were I to make the Games, I would be the youngest male swimmer to have qualified for a U.S. Olympic team since 1932, when thirteen-year-old Ralph Flanagan had made the team. In its 2000 Trials preview, *Swimming World* magazine said, "Fourteen-year-old Michael Phelps swam a phenomenal 1:59.02 at spring nationals but is probably a year or two from being a factor on the world scene."

The 2000 U.S. Olympic Trials were held in August in Indianapolis. The story that year heading into the meet was Dara Torres. At thirty-three, she was trying to become the first swimmer to win medals in four Olympics. Her first Olympics had been in 1984. That was the year before I was born.

I was hardly Dara Torres. I still had braces on my bottom teeth.

Bob and decided I would swim three races: the 200 fly, 200 IM, and 400 IM.

On the second day, in the 400 IM, I finished eleventh. Shake it off, Bob said. Let's focus on the 200 fly.

Malchow, the 1996 Olympic silver medalist and world record holder in 1:55.18, was the clear favorite. Three or four guys, including me, the third seed, were probably capable of going under 1:58. Up in the stands, the seats my family had gotten were crummy. Mom moved down to stand in a tunnel down by the diving well, an area where no standing was allowed. An usher told her to scoot. She said, "Just give me two minutes. Two minutes, two minutes, two minutes."

Before the race, Bob had told me that I'd probably be able to make up ground over the final 50 meters, per my style. Keep it close through the third turn, he said. Instead, at 150 meters. Mom started preparing an "I still love you" speech. Bob, too.

Over that last 50, I knew I was closing. But I had no idea whether I had closed enough. I touched. With my goggles on, I couldn't see the board right away, but I heard the announcer say my name and something about second place. I took the goggles off. The scoreboard said Malchow had come in first in 1:56.87. I was second, in 1:57.48.

My final 50 split had been nearly two seconds faster than Malchow's. He said on the pool deck, "I may have to retire sooner than I thought. He's exactly me four years ago. He doesn't know how much his life is going to change, but it's going to change real soon."

Not that much. Bob made sure of that.

The morning after making the 2000 Olympic team, I swam in a preliminary heat of the 200 IM at the Trials. The top sixteen made it to the next round; I finished twentieth.

•　　•　　•

In Sydney, for the first time in Olympic history, the U.S. women's swim team roster was older than the men's. Malchow had been the only teenager on the U.S. team in Atlanta. Now there were eight of us, five of whom would serve as mainstays for the American team for years to come:

Vendt was nineteen.

Ian Crocker and Klete Keller were eighteen.

Aaron Peirsol was seventeen.

And I was fifteen, still months away from even having a driver's license.

In Sydney, at the village, I roomed with Peirsol. He would go on to win silver in the 200 back.

In my first Olympic swim, I won my heat, in 1:57.30. In my semi, I lowered that to 1:57 flat. In both races, I swam with the strings of my suit untied. All I can say is, I was fifteen. The good news is, my suit didn't come off. The bad news is, it was like showing up for a job interview wearing a gray suit only to realize you had a blue sock on your left foot and a brown one on the right. A lack of preparation.

Bob had no access to the Olympic Village. At these Games, he was not formally a U.S. coach. He did have access to the pool deck from the people who ran Australian swimming. The times are okay, Michael, he told me. But these are the Olympic Games. You are going to treat them right. What did we say about preparation?

The next night, the plan was for me to leave the village early so I would get to the pool with, as they say in Australia, no worries. Bob wanted me there two-and-a-half hours before the race.

My cell phone rang.

"Hello."

"Hello, Bob."

"Michael, are you here at the pool?"

"No, I'm going back to the village."

"What? Now? Why?"

"I took the wrong credential. I was heading to the door and I grabbed Aaron's instead."

Bad. Very bad. Of course Bob was upset. To his credit, he did not yell.

"Well, okay," he said finally. "Let's get here and figure out what to do."

I got to the pool with a little bit more than an hour to go. We shortened my warm-up. I was jittery. When we walked out onto the deck, instead of doing my thing behind the block I walked over to Malchow to wish him luck. That's not the way it's done on the deck. I still don't know what I was thinking.

I swam that Olympic final in 1:56.50, a personal best, a time that would have won a medal at every previous Olympic final. It got me fifth. I was 33-hundredths of a second back of third place, and bronze.

Fifth. No medal.

Malchow won, in 1:55.35. He patted me on the back and said, "The best is ahead of you."

Bob sent me to the pool the next day for a workout. The workout sheet said, "Austin WR." That meant the 2001 spring nationals in Austin, Texas. No medal at the Olympics? New goal. World record in the 200 fly in Austin.

The final day of the swim meet in Sydney was medley relay day. I painted my face half red and half blue and wrote "Team USA" across my chest, and as I sat there, watching the American men and the American women win the medleys, I thought how cool it would be to swim the relays, which, at these Games, I had no chance of doing. At North Baltimore, I loved the feeling of being on a team. In Sydney, I loved it even more.

Maybe, I thought, in Athens.

And, I thought, maybe in Athens we could avenge the two freestyle relays, the 400 and the 800. Both were major American disappointments in Sydney, especially the 400.

Before Sydney, the United States had won the 400 each of the seven times it had been included on the Olympic program. The Australians wanted this one bad. It was in their country. The race was to be held on the first night of racing. They had Ian Thorpe, who at those Games would prove he was among the world's most dominant swimmers, assigned to the anchor leg. They were fired up, and then they got fired up even more because of Gary Hall, Jr., whose multiple Olympic medals included silver in the 100 free in 1996.

In an online diary published a month before the Olympics,

Gary had written how much he respected the Australian swim-mers. But he closed the article with a prediction that no one in Australia was soon going to forget: "We're going to smash them like guitars."

Everyone knew Gary would swim the anchor leg for the American team.

The rest was history.

An hour before the relay, Ian won the 400 free. He barely had time to change for the medals ceremony and then back into his bodysuit.

The Australians got out on the first leg. The Americans came back in the second. The Americans grabbed the lead in the first half of the third leg, but the Aussies came back. In the anchor leg, Gary passed Ian in the first length and turned six-tenths of a second ahead. With the home crowd roaring, Ian, who seemed so controlled, so languid almost in the water even as he was driving with ferocity to the wall, caught Gary with about 20 meters to go and edged ahead.

Ian knew when he touched that he had won. He sprang from the pool, and the Australians celebrated, with Michael Klim, who had taken the leadoff leg for the Aussies, memorably per-forming a mocking air-guitar concert on the deck.

"I doff my swimming cap to the great Ian Thorpe," Gary said later. "He had a better finish than I did."

I took it all in.

Lost in the commotion, at least for most people, was that third leg.

The American who swam that third leg: Jason Lezak.

● ● ●

The United States won thirty-three swimming medals in Sydney. Of the forty-eight swimmers on our team, forty-one came home with at least one medal. I was one of the seven who didn't.

In Austin the next spring, I got my world record. I defeated

Malchow and went 1:54.92 in the 200 fly. I had become the youngest male ever to hold a world record. I was fifteen years and nine months old. Thorpe had been the youngest before that, sixteen years and ten months.

Not accomplishing my goal in Sydney had driven me for all the months in between. I had always known how badly it hurt to lose, how much I hated it. Now I had concrete proof of how losing could motivate me to reach my goals at the highest levels of swimming.

The win in Austin earned me a trip to the 2001 world championships, in Fukuoka, Japan. I won the 200 fly—my first world title—and lowered the world record again, to 1:54.58.

That summer, I started to get asked more and more about the 2004 Olympics. If I could make the team, I said, I'd like the chance to medal in more than just one event. I was looking at the two flys, the 100 and 200, and the two medleys, the 200 and 400. This wasn't bragging. This was a reflection of how I had always trained, with an emphasis on versatility.

That summer, too, I signed an endorsement contract with Speedo. The deal was for four years, through 2005. I was barely sixteen, the youngest American male swimmer to turn professional.

It was about that time as well that, as I kept saying to Bob, why are all these people all of a sudden asking me about Mark Spitz?

Mark made himself legendary in Munich in 1972. But his excellence and potential had been apparent for years. In 1967, when he was seventeen, he won five gold medals at the Pan American Games in Mexico City. He then predicted he would win six golds at the 1968 Summer Games, again in Mexico City. He did win two golds, in the relays. But no more. In his last individual event, the 200 fly, he finished last.

Mark went to college at Indiana. In those days, there was no such thing as turning professional. There were no professionals at the Olympics then, and there had not been ever since the Games were revived in 1896, in Athens. In the ancient Games, way back when, at Olympia, winners got only an olive wreath; when the modern Olympics got started, it was with that ideal in mind. The rules of eligibility originally were driven by the notions of European aristocracy, in particular the idea that it would be cheap and undignified to play for pay. That's why Jim Thorpe was stripped of the medals he won in the pentathlon and the decathlon at the Olympics in 1912 in Stockholm; the year after the Games, he acknowledged he had earned $25 per week playing minor-league baseball in North Carolina in 1909 and 1910. By the strictest definition of the rules, he had been a professional athlete and therefore ineligible to compete at the Olympics.

The president of the IOC from 1952 through those Munich Olympics in 1972, Avery Brundage, an American, made the amateur code his official passion. It made no difference to Brundage that athletes in, say, the Soviet Union could get a commission in the army. If Spitz wanted to swim in Munich, to avenge his performance in 1968, he had to do so as an amateur. He could go to college, accept a scholarship, but that was it.

This story was all part of the lore of swimming.

And, as well, what happened in 1972.

First Mark won the 200 fly, beating, among others, Gary Hall, Sr. He anchored the winning 400 free relay. He won the 200 free, after which, waving to fans while holding a pair of tennis shoes, he got dragged before the IOC, and Brundage. Mark was accused by some of endorsing a product, which would have made him a professional. The IOC admonished Mark but did not ban him, the whole thing is a study in hypocrisy; on the Olympic grounds, the IOC was promoting the sale of special Games postcards bearing the images of Mark and other swim standouts.

He went back to the pool and got two more golds, in the 100 fly and 800 relay. He won the 100 free. The seventh gold came as he swam the butterfly leg of the medley relay.

Mark was not only the first to win seven golds.

He was the first to win six.

And then his career was over.

If he had been allowed to make money, it clearly would have been in his—not to mention, those hypothetical sponsors—interests to keep swimming. He could have gone to the 1976 Games in Montreal. Probably not swim seven events again. But he would have been only twenty-six, very much in his prime.

But he had no choice. He couldn't ponder the what-if, if I stayed in, how many more medals could I have won?

A few days after winning the seventh medal, Mark posed for a photo in his Speedo stars-and-stripes suit. It sold millions. That poster is probably one of those things that they'll find in one of those time capsules from the 1970s that got buried somewhere. Along with that one of Farrah Fawcett four years later.

Change to the Olympic eligibility code was very slow in coming. It didn't really happen until after 1981, when Juan Antonio Samaranch of Spain took over the IOC. It wasn't until 1985, the year I was born, that the international swimming federation—it's called FINA, after its French name, *Fédération Internationale de Natation*—began to allow swimmers to accept training stipends from their national federations. After the 1988 Seoul Olympics, under the direction of Samaranch, the IOC voted to accept professional athletes.

The IOC has since left eligibility rules up to the various international sports federations. Boxing chose to stick with amateurs. Soccer limits each team at the Olympics to three players over age twenty-three. The rest of the sports were only too glad to welcome professionals. Thus, for instance, the 1992 Olympics in Barcelona provided a worldwide stage for the Dream Team, the U.S. men's basketball all-star team that romped to the gold medal with Michael Jordan, Larry Bird, Magic Johnson, and the rest.

American swimmers who made the 1992 Olympic team were eligible to get a $1,500 monthly check from USA Swimming, plus a bonus of $1,250. The contrast with the Dream Teamers could not have been more dramatic.

That's why some swimmers set out to test the waters, so to speak.

I was very fortunate to be able to see an example of this first-hand. At North Baltimore, Anita Nall, who after winning those three medals in Barcelona was without question a star of our club, became the youngest American female swimmer to turn pro. But she did so without an agent. She maybe made $250,000 as a pro, mostly making speeches and working at swim clinics, and that was it.

Other swimmers did the college thing. Malchow went to Michigan. Jenny Thompson went to Stanford and starred at four Olympics, starting in 1992.

Bob, my mom, and I had started talking after Sydney about me turning pro; the world records in the 200 fly intensified the conversations; the records obviously increased my bargaining power. We all talked, too, about how important it would be to find not just an agent but the right agent, not just someone who would help find sponsors and negotiate contracts. The right agent would also be innovative and creative.

As we were having these discussions, I had not even begun my junior year of high school. I knew that if I turned pro I would be giving up the chance to compete for conference or NCAA championships, and might well not have the chance to experience the fraternity of college swimming. But what I was trying to do was bigger than conference or NCAA championships. I had already set a world record. I had already been to the Olympics. I had taken a hard look at my goals and realized I wanted more than college. Going pro would help me focus on meeting those goals.

I was on track to get my high school diploma in 2003. The Athens Olympics were in 2004. What was I going to do for that year? If I were a professional swimmer, the answer to that would be easy.

Yes, my high school classmates would be into and through their first year of college. Going pro would mean putting any formal education on the back burner. Then again, traveling the world because of swimming might offer me the equivalent of graduate-level courses in business, marketing, and international relations.

I have always done my swimming in a Speedo suit.

That first deal with Speedo, signed in 2001, went through 2005. It included a clause that would pay for my college education if my swimming career didn't work out.

Obviously, I had promise, but was still very much a work in progress. About a month after the news broke that I had turned pro, I traveled to the U.S. Open short-course meet in Long Island. Walking onto the deck to swim the 200 back, I realized I had forgotten my cap and goggles. I looked at my mom. She shrugged her shoulders. I shrugged mine. I looked at Bob. Same thing.

I had to learn to change from being a kid to a professional. They say you learn more from your mistakes than anything.

• • •

If it seemed obvious, it was no less imperative to find an agent with Olympic experience. But whom?

The Salt Lake City Winter Olympics took place in February 2002. Bob was watching the *Today* show one morning when Matt Lauer introduced an agent named Peter Carlisle. Two of his snowboarding clients, Ross Powers and Kelly Clark, had won the halfpipe events in Salt Lake; Peter was on the show explaining strategies to reach young people interested in action sports, music, computer games. Bob put down his coffee cup.

This, he thought, is the guy.

It took two months to hold a meeting, as Peter was just too busy looking after his stars from those Winter Games. He was director of Olympic sports for Octagon, an agency based outside Washington, D.C., that had acquired his independent agency the year before. His home base was in Maine, where he grew up.

"So," Peter said to me at that first meeting, "what do you want for your future, Michael? What are your goals?"

I said the first thing that came to mind: "I want to change the sport of swimming."

In Australia, swimmers were on billboards, in commercials. Kids grow up there wanting to be swimmers the way they grow up in the United States wanting to play quarterback. In Australia, swimming was often the lead topic on the nightly news—not just the sports segment, the entire news show. How often was swimming even shown on a sports highlight show in the United States?

I was still sixteen years old. I wasn't trying to be overbearing. I truly did not think I was that full of myself. I had been asked a question and was trying to answer it honestly.

"I want to change the sport of swimming, I want people to talk about it, think about it, and look forward to seeing it. I want them to want to jump in and do it. That's my goal."

I signed up with Peter that summer. He negotiated a deal with Visa that put me in line to make me one of the athletes it would feature in the run-up to the 2004 Olympics. And then he waited.

Peter has a guilty pleasure: reality television. He was fascinated by the dynamics of *Survivor*. What does the winner of *Survivor* get?

A $1 million check.

The first meet of mine that Peter saw in person came in the summer of 2002, the summer nationals in Fort Lauderdale, Florida. The meet, the U.S. qualifier for the 2003 Worlds in Barcelona, ended with me being the first man since Spitz to hold four American records. The next year, in Barcelona, I became the first swimmer to lower world records in different events on the same day.

While in Barcelona, the time had come. Peter asked to meet with Speedo's executives. He said, we need to renegotiate the contract, for all the right reasons.

What, they asked, do you want?

He said, a million bucks. If, in Athens, Michael matches Spitz's seven golds, you pay him a million bucks.

There were other details—a base salary, smaller bonuses for some lesser number of medals in Athens, and so on—but the million was the nut of the deal. Think, Peter told the company's executives, of the publicity this would bring not just Michael, but Speedo.

Incentive deals are common in pro football and baseball. You make the Pro Bowl, you get an extra $100,000. You make baseball's All-Star team, here's $50,000. Or whatever. This simply extended an idea that had become commonplace in other sports to swimming.

Carmelo Anthony went to high school a mile away from where I did. He spent one year in college, leading Syracuse to an NCAA championship. Then he was drafted by the Denver Nuggets. In July 2003, the Nuggets signed him to a four-year, $15.1 million contract. Five days later, I dove into the water for my first heat in the 200 fly at the Worlds in Barcelona. If I was in swimming solely to make money, I was in the wrong sport.

And this: Carmelo was going to be on television dozens of times that fall. Swimming wasn't going to be seen live on any American television network during all of 2003.

My Speedo deal, with the $1 million bonus, was announced in November 2003 and, from then on, I had to navigate a balance.

It wasn't until the Fort Lauderdale meet the year before that Bob had even allowed himself to think I might have the capability to reach for seven medals.

In fact, it had been such a nonstarter that, asked about it early in the meet by a reporter from the Colorado Springs newspaper— the U.S. Olympic Committee is based there, and so what's written by the local paper, the *Gazette,* gets noticed by Olympic insiders everywhere—Bob almost snorted. "You can compare Michael to Mark Spitz in that he swims a lot of different events in different strokes at a high level," he said. "Now can he win seven events, seven gold medals? That's very difficult to do in this day and age.

". . . I can't imagine right now we'd try an event program that would be that ambitious."

Still, Bob said, "I'm not going to rule it out."

I had told the same reporter it might be fun to aim for. "It's harder now than it was back then. If you can do it, wow!"

Bob was having no more *wow* talk. As soon as the thought of seven came up, he shoved it right back down. The way to think about seven medals wasn't to talk about it. It was to train.

The bonus, predictably, generated enormous publicity. That was good. But complex.

It was essential never to be disrespectful of any of my teammates or rivals. Not that I ever would. I simply had to be aware of the dynamic. Each of them had goals, too.

It was key to be respectful in everything I said and did about Mark. That was easy. What he did was amazing. It deserves enormous respect. He has, always has had, mine.

It was also critical to separate myself from Mark. I wasn't trying to be him. I was me. And what I wanted, what I was after, was to do something no one else had done. That's what I set my mind to, and that's what I was going for.

It's not a lie that I wanted to beat the record. It's not a secret. I just wasn't going to come out and say it. Why would I? The only person who could help me accomplish my goals was Bob. No offense to anyone in the media, but is a reporter going to help me swim faster? A reporter going to help me win any medal of any kind? That's why I kept everything to myself. It wasn't necessary to share my goals with anyone but Bob. So I didn't do it.

If I was asked, can you beat Spitz? I might say, you never know what can happen. I would then go on to say, the only person I can worry about is myself. If I can prepare the best I can, that's all I can ask. If I go in and still get beat with my best time, that's all I can ask for. I can't say yes or no.

To answer, well, of course I want to beat him and I think I can, would be impolite and immodest. It would be trash-talking. Not my way.

My goals were my goals, and they were to win as many as I could win. If everything broke right, I could win a number that, as it turns out, rhymes with the word "fate." Bob and I planned it. He said: You have the ability to swim these events at a high level. Show the world what you can do. Never mind the world. Show yourself.

We called it Plan A.

•   •   •

To see Plan A to its completion, I had to swim relays.

A major international swim meet lasts eight days. Even so, there are only so many individual events that it would be possible, even in theory, to swim, because race finals are sometimes scheduled one after the other, sometimes within minutes.

If I was to break into the 400 relay, that meant I had to, among other things, start swimming faster in the 100 free. I was told in Barcelona, and this was by one of the guys on our team, you'll never break 50 seconds.

I didn't say anything back. Everyone would learn, eventually, that, aside from losing itself, nothing made me more determined than when someone doubted me.

At the 2003 summer nationals in College Park, Maryland, just down the road from Baltimore, I won the 100 free in 49.19. Six months later, in Orlando, at the spring nationals, I won again, in 49.05, even though my reaction time off the blocks, 1.21 seconds, was awful, and I was dead last at the turn. In Santa Clara, California, in the spring of 2004, Jason and I raced head-to-head in the 100; I won.

I did not compete in the 100 free at the 2004 Trials. Jason won, in 48.41, ahead of Ian Crocker, in 49.06. Gary Hall, Jr. was just behind Ian, in 49.16. In fourth: Neil Walker, who for years had been one of the most reliable American relay guys.

In seventh place at those 2004 Trials: Garrett Weber-Gale.

Because I didn't swim in the 100 free at the Trials, of course there was some tension that revolved around whether I should get to swim in the 400 relay in Athens. It surfaced immediately in Long Beach.

I didn't swim the race at the Trials because I didn't have to. The fact is, any member of an Olympic team can be used in the relay. My 49.05 in Orlando was faster than Ian had gone at the Trials. I had beaten Jason in Santa Clara.

Obviously, though, if I swam, someone else was not going to.

At that point, Gary had eight Olympic medals. He had experience and pride. Having been beaten by Thorpe in the 400 relay final in Sydney, he was naturally seeking another chance. His point, as he told reporters, was, "Somebody swam the 100 free and earned a spot on that relay. You're talking about a lifetime of work. I'm supportive of Michael and his goals. I want to see the relay win gold. It's only fair for the individuals who earned a place on the relay to swim in the Olympics. Four of us are swimming for one spot if Michael's there."

The answer came from Eddie Reese, the U.S. men's coach. Our American men hadn't won a major international relay since 1998. Eddie, like Gary—like me, like all of us—wanted to win in Athens. When we got there, he said, somebody had to swim a split time of 48.2 or 48.3, roughly equivalent to a sub-49 time in an individual 100 free, to grab one of the spots in the final; a 48.2 or 48.3 relay split would trump the 49.05 I had done in Orlando. If fewer than two did so, I would swim with Ian and Jason, who by virtue of going one-two at the Trials had clinched two of the spots.

"I want Michael Phelps in as many events as possible," Eddie said, "and in as many as he can do well."

When we got to Athens, Neil swam a 48.16 split in the prelims. He got a spot in the finals. Gary went 48.73. He did not.

I know Gary didn't like not being on that relay in the finals, but you're not going to like everything that happens in life.

Ian, Neil, Jason and me, and I asked to swim leadoff. Bob asked that I swim leadoff. That's where I would feel the most comfortable.

Two reasons: I like being able to get an early lead, and I thought I could.

Also, for the guy going second, third, or fourth, the timing of leaving the blocks is an intricate thing. The ultimate goal is to time the dive so that you're horizontal to the water surface, but with your feet still in contact with the blocks, as the swimmer in the water is making his touch.

The coaching staff went with a different order: Ian, me, Neil, Jason.

Ian went first. He was fifth at the turn. And then he just didn't have it. He touched in 50.05, dead last, and what turned out to be the slowest time of any of the thirty-two guys in the field.

I swam 48.74. That got us into sixth. Neil went 47.97, the fastest split of his career, to get us to third. Jason swam furiously and for a moment we were in second. But he was passed in the closing meters by Pieter van den Hoogenband of the Netherlands.

The South Africans won in world-record time, 3:13.17. The Dutch came in second, in 3:14.36. We finished third, in 3:14.62. It was the worst American showing ever in an Olympic 400 free relay.

"I'm sorry. It's my fault. It's my fault," Ian said.

"Dude, this is one race," I told him.

Gary did not even show up to watch. Word was that he stayed in the village.

Eddie, meanwhile, apparently did not know that Ian, who

had swum in college for Eddie at the University of Texas, was sick, with a runny nose and a sore throat.

That race, which came on just the second day of the meet, abruptly ended any notions of going beyond seven gold medals in Athens. At the start of the Games, I had watched the movie *Miracle,* the story of the 1980 U.S. Olympic hockey team. Now, it looked as though I might need to call on a miracle of my own if I had any hope of seeing Plan A through; I would have to win all six of my remaining events, and in some of those events—the 200 free, in particular—I would not be the favorite.

But that's not why the walk off the pool deck that night was a long one. It would be a long four years until we could again claim that relay gold for the United States, where it belonged.

• • •

The time I put up in Omaha in the 100 free prelims at the 2008 Trials, 47.92, tied Garrett's winning time in the Trials finals. This time around, there wasn't any question as to whether I was deserving; there would be no controversy about whether I ought to be one of the four swimming the 400 relay finals at the Olympics.

Garrett, after that seventh-place finish in the 2004 Trials, had steadily been improving, training in Texas with Eddie, whom Garrett's dad calls the "Zen master of swimming." For years, Eddie has been telling Garrett he has the gift of the kick. Eddie would keep telling Garrett: Kick! Kick! It wasn't until the Beijing Olympics were in sight, in the spring of 2008, that Garrett finally got it. Going into the Trials and then onto Beijing, you could tell Garrett was mentally just right there. Garrett is something of a foodie—he loves restaurants and collects recipes for dishes like smoky salmon jerky—but had been working all year with a nutritionist and had been on a low-sugar, low-protein diet. He kept saying that the rigorous diet was in part to help train his mind; he said it made him feel like he had an edge and was ready to go. If you don't expect to do well, he kept saying at the Trials, you're not going to swim fast. In Omaha, Garrett won both the 100 and the 50. He was swimming fast, even setting an American record of 21.47 in the 50, after which he treated himself to dessert for the first time in nearly three months: one raspberry sorbet.

Jason was swimming fast, too, going 47.58, also an American record, at the Trials in the 100 semifinals. And Jason was thirty-two years old. Just to compare: At the Trials, Garrett was twenty-two, I turned twenty-three during the meet, Cullen was twenty-four, and here was Jason, at thirty-two, still bringing it strong. Jason and I had been hanging out together on national teams since Sydney, but there was something different about him this time around. He was more relaxed and more social this year than I had ever seen him before. Not that he wasn't relaxed or social before, but it was obvious that he was appreciating what we had this time, an unbelievable sense of team and of camaraderie.

At the Olympic Village, I was put into a six-person suite with Lochte, Jones, Shanteau, Vendt, and Gil Stovall. Shanteau had made the 2008 team in the 200 breast; Vendt had made it for the prelims of the 800-meter free relay; Stovall was an up-and-comer in the 200 fly. Jason would come into our suite at the village and hang out while we were playing card games; Lochte and I would be taking on Cullen and Shanteau in spades. Jason would just soak it all in, would sit there, a big part of it all, all of us laughing and appreciating the moment and each other.

The sense of togetherness on this 2008 U.S. men's Olympic swim team will forever be one of my great memories from Beijing. In the pool, we had to compete. Outside of it, we were not just teammates but brothers. Every single one of us.

Before the Olympics started, we held an athletes-only meeting. No coaches. Some of us who had been at prior Games told the new guys about those memories. About how some of the best moments come away from the pool. About how being on the American swim team is one of the biggest honors anyone could ever have. About trying to savor not just the competition but the experience.

And about some of our goals for the Olympics, one of which was crystal clear: Take back the 400 relay gold.

Jason, in particular, was tired of losing. He swam the third leg on the 2000 relay, the anchor in 2004. Silver and bronze. He wanted gold.

And now comes Bob, the morning of the race, to say the French are trash-talking? They're going to smash us like guitars? Gary's words from 2000, now thrown in our face?

When I heard that, it was like a switch flipped in my body, like, you really want to do that? We didn't need any more motivation. But we had just gotten it.

I said to Jason at breakfast, you hear what the French are saying?

He just smiled.

Bob and I saw Garrett on his way back from breakfast. Hey, guess what the French said?

I don't want to hear it, Garrett said. We'll take care of business when we get out to the pool.

We got to the pool pretty fired up. And then we got fired up more.

In the hallway outside the ready room, the four of us got together in a football huddle. The talk immediately turned raw and emotional.

Jason said he had been on losing relays before. I'm not, he said, going to let it happen again. This, he said, is not a 4x100 relay, four guys each swimming a 100. There's nothing here about swimming a leg individually. This is a 400 relay; we're all together. We're all going to be one. He said we have to prepare ourselves and go out there and kick it.

We were like: Yeah, yeah, yeah. Bouncing up and down. Ready to rock. Fired up.

Out on the deck, in introductions, nobody said a word. Nobody had to. We drew next to each other and raised our hands up in unison. A team. Together.

This was obviously going to be a super-fast race. Six of the eight teams in the final had gone faster in the 2008 prelims than the South Africans had done in winning the 2004 relay in Athens in a then-world record 3:13.17. Including the South Africans, who were back with the same four guys.

The Australians had Eamon Sullivan, the world-record holder in the 50 and a complete threat in the 100. They were for sure going to swim fast.

The French had three guys who had come on in the last year, one of them Bernard, the 100 world-record holder with that 47.5. He had broken the 100 record twice in March. They would swim fast.

Bring it on.

We were ready to rock, ready to swim fast, too.

Faster.

Until this moment, five guys in the entire world had gone under 48 seconds in an open 100 this year. Bernard, Sullivan, and three Americans: Garrett, Jason, and me.

The pressure had to be on the French. They had never won a medal in the event. They were trying to win France's first swimming relay gold.

I got up on the block, above Lane 4. My guys behind me were calling, come on, Mike! Come on, Phelps! Lead it off! Step it up! Let's go! I started to get chills.

The beep sounded.

I knew the French guy, Amaury Leveaux, second-fastest ever in the 50, was going to be out quick. The plan was to stay with him. He was in Lane 5, to my left. Sullivan, the Australian, was to my right, in Lane 3.

At 25 meters, halfway down the first length, I saw that Sullivan was already half a body length ahead of me. If I want to have a good split, I thought at the turn, I have got to win this leg.

Bang-bang-bang. In the relays, you're in the water and just that fast, you're out. I didn't win the leg. I had put us in second place, behind the Australians, and Sullivan. But I knew I had turned in a good leg. I had no idea about anyone's times, mine, anyone's. As soon as I touched I got out of the pool and got back behind our lane. I started cheering like no one has ever cheered before.

Garrett, in his first Olympic swim, moved us up to first. He overtook Australia's Andrew Lauterstein; the Aussies slipped back to third. Swimming second for the French was Fabien Gilot, who, going into the race, had put down the sixth-fastest time in the world that year in the 100; he moved France up into second at 200. Less than a second separated all three teams.

Cullen took off. So did France's Bousquet. We all knew about Bousquet. He spent four years, from 2001 to 2005, swimming for Auburn. He had an immense tattoo on his left shoulder. He was also no-doubt-about-it fast; with the flying starts the relays allow, he had gone 46.63 in the prelims the night before. That was the fastest relay split in history.

Bousquet poured it on. He took the lead going toward the far wall.

Cullen hung tough.

Bousquet touched. Bernard leaped into the water.

Cullen touched. Jason dove off after him. When they surfaced, Jason looked to be about half a body length behind.

Bernard, in his white cap, roared toward the far wall. Jason, to his right, hung to the left lane line. Technically perfect. So smart. He was riding in behind the wave that Bernard, who is 6-feet-5, was making in Lane 5.

At the final turn, Bernard was 82-hundredths ahead, almost a full length.

If anyone else was starting to give up hope, Garrett, Cullen, and

I were giving up nothing. We believed. Cullen, who had just finished his leg, was jumping up and down by the side of the pool. The noise level inside the Cube by now was furious. Garrett and I started screaming: Get this guy!

Behind the blocks, we could see that after his turn Bernard had made a stupid, and what would turn out to be colossal, mistake. After the flip, instead of swimming in the middle of his lane, he had drifted to the left. That meant that Jason, now to Bernard's left, could again tuck in behind him. Bernard was doing the hard work. Jason was cruising, preparing to slingshot by Bernard.

And Jason was starting to close. Jason would say later that when he turned and saw how far ahead Bernard was, he thought, no way; coming into the race, Bernard was the fastest guy in the world in the 100. But then, Jason said, he immediately thought, you know what, that is ridiculous. I'm here for my guys. I'm here for the United States of America. I don't care how bad it hurts. I'm just going to go out there and hit it. Jason thought all this in a split second. He got, as he described it, a super-charge, more adrenaline than he'd ever had. It was electric. The moment was electric.

Jason started swimming as if he were possessed. Bernard began to falter. He was suddenly tight. Overswimming it. Maybe his hellacious first 50 had left him without enough to finish.

Get this guy!

Garrett started pounding on the block.

We both were screaming. Big time.

Get this guy!

Jason closed some more. With each stroke, he was gaining. Clearly he was going to catch Bernard, if only he had enough pool left to do it.

With about 15 meters left, it suddenly looked like Jason would have enough pool.

Jason and Bernard churned toward the finish.

I was smacking the block. Smacking that block. Smacking it. Screaming. Garrett, to my right, was screaming.

Jason lunged toward the wall.

Garrett and I looked across the pool, at the big board.

Yes!

Next to the number 1, it said: United States.

Jason had touched first, in 3:08.24. The French were second, eight-hundredths behind. U-S-A! Victory!

I punched the air with my right fist. I threw both my arms up, touchdown style. Garrett put his arm around me for just a moment as I leaned back and screamed with everything I had. Garrett moved just a step away and flexed like he was Arnold Schwarzenegger in the 1970s.

I reached down and slapped Jason's hands in the water. I turned to the stands to my left, arched my back, and roared again. I had never been so excited in my entire life.

Cullen came over from the side of the pool. He and I had a fast hug. Jason climbed out of the water and hugged Garrett. All four of us got together and embraced, formed a huddle, like the one just a few minutes before in the hall outside the ready room. Way to go, guys, I said. We did it. That relay is ours again.

The huddle broke. "That's what I'm talking about!" I yelled.

Bernard was still in the pool. He had heaved his elbows onto the deck. He was just hanging there, heaving, exhausted, disappointed.

One of the French racers, Gilot, said afterward, *"C'est le sport,"* which means literally, "It's sport," but in this context really meant, "That's why you race the race."

Jason had just thrown down the fastest relay split in history, 46.06 seconds. "America," Jason would say later, "has a great tradition of winning that relay. All of us knew what we're capable of, but to actually do it, to get that tradition back, it's a phenomenal feeling. Still, right now, I'm in disbelief."

All of us were. Later, when we ran the numbers, all we could say was: unbelievable, and incredible.

Our time, 3:08.24, was almost exactly four full seconds faster than the world record that Nathan, Cullen, Ben, and Matt had gone in the prelims. It had taken eighteen years, from the Seoul Olympics in 1988 until 2006, for the record to drop four seconds to the 3:12 range. Nathan, Cullen, Ben and Matt had cut another two-tenths of a second off the mark; now we had dropped it, the very next day, nearly four full seconds. Incredible.

Five of the eight teams in the relay final swam under the mark that Nathan, Cullen, Ben and Matt had set in the prelims. The Australians took bronze. The Swedes and Italians also went under what had been that world record time, and got nothing. No medal. Unbelievable.

My first-leg split, 47.51, was a new American record, just one-hundredth of a second off what had been the world record going into the race. That time was a personal best by 41-hundredths. It was just one-hundredth off my goal sheet time.

I had turned the race over to Garrett with us in second only because Sullivan, two lanes over, had set a new world record, 47.24. Two days later, Bernard would go 47.20, only to be out-done again, this time by Sullivan, 47.05.

The four of us Americans walked over to the NBC broadcast position on the deck. Andrea Kremer, the network's poolside reporter throughout the Olympics in Beijing, got us all together in front of the camera.

"Well," she said, "the French had said we're gonna smash the Americans. Who's talking now, guys?"

"We are," Garrett said. "United States of America."

This relay had loomed as one of the toughest races for me if I were to make it to eight. Thanks to my teammates, maybe, in Beijing in 2008, my dreams really could come true. There was a lot of swimming yet to go, an unforeseeable future. But maybe.

Jason couldn't have been more gracious. "I think Michael knows we didn't do this for him," he said. "He was just a part of it. We were a part of it."

Cullen, too. "He's on a mission to win eight and we're happy to be a part of it."

And Garrett. "And we wanted one of these, too," he said, meaning the gold medals they gave us when we had ascended the podium, arms together, to celebrate a race that the president of the United States had watched us win. President Bush had been back in the stands at the Cube.

The president told reporters that he had been watching me as Jason touched, watched my exuberance and joy. "The whole thing is genuine," President Bush said. "That's the good thing about the Olympics."

I have been asked many, many times since whether, because Jason's extraordinary effort kept alive my shot at the $1 million bonus, I said something to Jason about it, or his effort. The answer is no. There were no words, except for those Jason said himself: "People always step up and do things out of the ordinary at the Olympics."

3

REDEMPTION:
THE 200 FREESTYLE

When the $1 million bonus play was being studied and weighed, all of us knew that winning seven golds against world-class competition, much less eight, meant everything would have to break the right way.

That said, it was far from impossible.

Was I setting myself up for media hype? Absolutely.

Would I be perceived as a failure in some quarters if I didn't reach eight or seven? No doubt.

Would it nonetheless create unprecedented buzz for swimming? For sure, and that made the decision to go forward easy.

There are two ways to look at the hype and the attention. You can look at it as a negative, as pressure. Or you can look at it as a positive, as support.

I got those lines from Ian Thorpe. In response to any question about attention, those lines served as his standard response.

After a while, I learned to make the answer more my own. I'm glad people are interested, I would say. I don't look at it as pressure, only as expectations, but the only expectations I focus on are those I have for myself, because those are the only ones I can do something about.

In practice, I sometimes pass the time doing laps by singing in my head the last song I heard in the car on the way to the pool.

I got that from Ian Thorpe.

There was a lot I could learn from Ian Thorpe, the least of which had to do with swimming.

I have always looked up to Michael Jordan, the way he changed his sport, just the way I want to help change swimming. Ian, in Australia, was like Michael Jordan. The man.

When, in Fukuoka, Japan, in 2001, I won my first world title, in the 200 fly, Ian was in the midst of winning the 200, 400, and 800 freestyles, all in world-record time; he also anchored the Australian team to victory in all three relays. Ian's three world records came in four days; the six gold medals came in seven events—he finished fourth in the 100 free—and amounted to the most any male had won at a major international meet since Spitz, in 1972. My world record at that meet, in the 200 fly, had actually been the second one set on the night I swam; Ian had broken the record in the 400 free. At the Olympics in Sydney the year before, Ian had won five medals, three of them gold. In Fukuoka, he was even better. The day after I broke that mark in the 200 fly, a newspaper headline screamed, "Teenage Stars Thorpe, Phelps Break Records." Ian was eighteen, turning nineteen that October. I was barely sixteen. He was the star, the main attraction. And, at first, it was hard to think I had business being in the same headline—in some regards, at least at that point, even in the same pool. One day, warming up, Ian slipped into the water and blew by; he made up what seemed like 20 meters on me in two strokes.

Of all the records that Ian set in Fukuoka, the one that was without a doubt most impressive came in the 200 free. In Sydney, Ian had lost the 200 free to Pieter van den Hoogenband, Pieter touching in 1:45.35, which tied Pieter's own world record. At the Australian championships the next March, Ian went 1:44.69. In Fukuoka, he went 1:44.06. That time seemed ungodly fast, a record that might last for years, maybe a decade or more. At least that's what van den Hoogenband said, and most everyone who knew anything about swimming, and the limits of human performance, agreed.

While Ian was magnificent in the pool, he was a study in how to behave out of it.

What composure. At a press conference in Fukuoka, he was asked if he could recite words he had learned in Japanese; he responded with a list of about thirty, the list including words and phrases that weren't related to each other. The follow-up question came: could he recite the same list in English? Ian did so, just as he had done in Japanese, not making even a single slip in the sequence.

Bob unabashedly used Ian as a model for my development. That made sense. There were remarkable parallels.

Ian had started swimming because his big sister did, like me with my older sisters. I didn't want to put my face in the water at first; he was initially thought to be allergic to chlorine. Ian's sister, Christina, and mine, Whitney, competed at the 1995 Pan Pacific Championships; neither made the 1996 Olympics. Ian's mom was a schoolteacher; mine was a teacher, later a principal. Ian was twelve when Doug Frost became his coach; I was eleven when Bob arrived at North Baltimore. He grew to be 6-feet-4; me, too. The 200 fly in Austin in 2001 made me the youngest male to set a world record; Ian had been the youngest before me. Moreover, Ian was the youngest world champion ever, just three months past his fifteenth birthday when he won the 400 free at the 1998 worlds.

The pressure on Ian at the 2000 Olympics was intense; he was one of the country's biggest heroes in a nation where the majority of people live within a few miles of the water, seemingly everyone swims, and the Olympic effort in swimming is grossly out of proportion to its population. There are about 20 million people in Australia, compared to more than 300 million in the United States. Even so, going back decades, Australians have been winning swimming medals at the Olympics in bunches. At the 1956 Summer Games in Melbourne, Aussies won every event in freestyle, the Australian crawl. At the Sydney Games, with those five medals, Ian more than delivered; he was chosen to be the Australian flag-bearer in the closing ceremony.

An explosion of patriotic excitement enveloped Australia when Ian won the 400 at the Sydney Games. He was just seventeen; the 400 final was held on the first night of competition; the place was jammed with his countrymen; he led from start to finish; and he set a world record, 3:40.59. There's a photo of Ian touching at the finish, so far ahead of everyone, that Bob had framed. The moment was so moving for Bob that, in Ann Arbor, he hung the photo in a place of honor, over his piano.

Three nights after that 400, Ian came in second in the 200 free, behind van den Hoogenband. To all of Australia, this was a huge surprise. To Ian, too. Backstage at the Sydney Games, Bob had gone into a bathroom moments after that 200 free final; Ian walked in a moment later. For maybe a beat or two after he walked in, Ian looked totally in shock. But that's why he had gone into the bathroom, to compose himself, away from everyone and everything. It took just a moment. He and Bob saw each other, acknowledged each other's presence, and Bob said, "Hey, good job." Ian replied, "Thanks," and went out to meet the press.

Ian had been a public figure in Australia since he was fourteen. He was clever enough to copyright his nickname, "Thorpedo." He was active in charity work. He struck endorsement deals with major corporate interests. At the Sydney Olympics, you couldn't cross the street, it seemed, without seeing Ian's face on a billboard, couldn't watch television without seeing Ian in a commercial; he had contracts with, among others, an airline and a bank. Later, he would have his own underwear line. Ian had interests in fashion and culture and moved easily within those circles everywhere in the world, especially in New York City; he was in New York on the morning of September 11, 2001, and had stopped at the World Trade Center on a morning run before going back to his hotel. He went on to help try to promote New York City's unsuccessful bid for the 2012 Summer Olympics.

In Australia, Ian was a star among stars. A couple of years after the Worlds in Fukuoka, a Sydney newspaper held a contest: Who would you like to invite to your home for Christmas? Russell Crowe finished fourth, Nicole Kidman third, then-Prime Minister John Howard second. Ian won.

Like many Aussies, Ian has always had a candor about him. In January 2008, in Beijing for the formal opening of the Water Cube, Ian was asked there by reporters whether that summer I could win eight gold medals.

"I don't think he will do it but I'd love to see it," Ian said. "There's a thing called competition. It won't just be one athlete that will be competing, and in a lot of events he has a lot of strong competition."

Bob, always sleuthing, knew I would be keen to read Ian's opinion.

At the Michigan pool, I had a collection of suits, caps, goggles, towels, and water bottles in my locker, all of it stashed around a big hook hanging from the locker top. After reading the sheet of paper with Ian's remarks, I took that paper and jammed it right onto that hook.

It stayed there all that winter, all that spring, into the summer, until we went to Omaha and the Trials. Every day when I'd open that locker, it was the first thing I'd see, that article, Ian's words, dangling there. Every day when I'd close that locker door, that fluttering piece of paper served as a reminder of the many doubters.

• • •

One of my early training tools consisted of videotape that Bob had picked up. It was of Ian overtaking Grant Hackett, another Australian, to win that 400 free at the 1998 worlds. Ian's stokes, so fluid, managed somehow to combine economy and power. His freestyle kick, with his size-17 feet, was like a motor. Unreal. I started trying to make my kick more like his, to make it as powerful as I could. Then there was his dolphin kick, which was nothing less than revolutionary. At turns, instead of pushing off the wall and then surfacing, he would stay underwater, where there was less resistance than up top, for several meters, his feet and legs moving together instead of kicking separately, the motion creating an incredible whip through the water that mimicked the movements of a dolphin.

The videotape, a grainy VHS thing, veered from the race to a poolside interview that Ian conducted immediately afterward. I also studied the way Ian talked, the way he held his hands, where he looked.

It was all part of Bob's effort to get me to be serious. I got serious.

The rules say you're allowed to kick underwater off the turn for a full 15 meters. During the summer of 2002, Bob and I resolved to work that dolphin kick into my training, into my IM sets. If we did ten 400 IMs, for instance, I would dolphinkick on the last two, from breast to free; then work my way up to four, six, eight, and, finally, ten.

At those 2002 summer nationals in Fort Lauderdale, I saw for the first time at a big meet what a weapon that dolphin kick could be. A month beforehand, Vendt had beaten me in a 400 IM; that would be the last time I would lose, a streak I carried into and through the Olympics in Athens and Beijing. In Fort Lauderdale, Erik turned first at 350; I stayed under for another 12 meters before breaking the surface. Watching a video of the race afterward, I could see that Erik had taken five full strokes before I even broke the surface. At the finish, I got the touch. Both of us finished in under world-record time, me in 4:11.09, Erik in 4:11.27.

Because I was naturally a butterflyer, the dolphin kick was relatively easy to pick up. In the IMs, it became an equalizer; even if other guys had a better breaststroke, I could use the dolphin on the turns. If they were getting tired on that final leg, I still had something to unleash.

Just three days after that meet ended, we went to the Pan Pacs, back in Japan, this time in Yokohama. I finished with three gold medals and two silvers. After the last race, I got on a bus, and there was Ian. We talked about this and that and, at one point, he said, if you ever want to train together, I'd be more than happy to have you in Australia. I was pumped. To be able to train with Ian Thorpe—cool. Think of what I'd learn. Hey, I said, and you can train with me in Baltimore, too.

When we got off the bus that night, no one paid any attention to me; those who had been waiting pushed by me to get a glimpse of Ian.

Bob spent a fair amount of time over the next six months trying to coordinate flights, pool times, training schedules, even an appearance at a training clinic in Australia. A week before we were to go, Ian's new coach, Tracy Menzies, e-mailed to say they were backing out. Something had come up, we were told.

This was a major disappointment.

There were other disappointments along the way as well.

We still went to Australia, where I trained with Hackett. Trained hard. For example, we raced each other over 50 meters, with and without fins, thirty times. We raced each other with pulleys. We raced freestyle; no wonder the Aussies were such great freestylers.

While there, Bob and I agreed to speak to what we were told would be a couple of reporters; there ended up being more than three dozen. We mentioned in passing that our morning practice the next day would be open to anyone who wanted to watch. We got to the pool at five-thirty in the morning. It was raining. We didn't expect to see a soul. The deck was jammed, a mass of people end to end. This was what swimming was all about in Australia. Why couldn't it be like this in the United States?

Grant, and Ian, and others had taken a sport that was already at the top in their country and moved it even farther along. As a sign of my profound respect, I wanted to measure myself against them even more after the trip Down Under than before. It was unlikely I would ever race against Grant; he was pursuing distance events, I was not. But to compete against Ian would be the ultimate. The 2003 Worlds in Barcelona would be coming up soon enough.

●   ●   ●

Bob's coaching philosophy can be distilled as follows:

Set your goals high. Work conscientiously, every day, to achieve them.

Among the many authors Bob has read, he likes to cite the motivational speaker Earl Nightingale, who survived the attack on Pearl Harbor on the USS *Arizona,* then went on to a career in broadcasting. The way Bob tells it, Nightingale's work revealed the one thing that's common to all successful people: They make a habit of doing things that unsuccessful people don't like to do.

That's it. That's Bob's game. His drill, while sometimes fabulously complex, is really quite simple—make a habit of doing things others weren't willing to do.

There are plenty of people with some amount of talent. Are you willing to go farther, work harder, be more committed and dedicated than anyone else?

If others were inclined to take Sunday off, well, that just meant we might be one-seventh better.

For five years, from 1998 to 2003, we did not believe in days off. I had one because of a snowstorm, two more due to the removal of wisdom teeth. Christmas? See you at the pool. Thanksgiving? Pool. Birthdays? Pool. Sponsor obligations? Work them out around practice time.

On September 11, 2001, I reported to afternoon practice at Meadowbrook. Bob began the session, which ultimately ended early, with a defiant pep talk. We don't stop for snow, for rain, for a flood, and we for sure aren't going to stop for terrorists, he declared. Terrorists might kill innocent Americans but not our dreams. They want us to sit home and be scared. That, he said, is not us.

During those years, Bob figured, counting meets, that I could work in the pool about 550 times each year. In all, between Sydney and Athens, about 2,200 times, enough to swim somewhere around 9,000 miles.

I loved it when people who have no clue—mostly guys I knew from high school who had played other sports—would say to me, swimming can't be that hard. Okay, I would say, why don't you come do our workout for a day?

I knew I could get by in whatever workout anyone else might have. I could run. I could catch. I could play defense in football or lacrosse. I could kick a soccer ball, hit a baseball.

I guarantee you, I would say, there is not a chance you would make it through even my warm-up.

Yeah, right, dude, they'd say.

Then come, I'd say.

No one ever did.

To understand how much more difficult it is to move through water than it is through air, consider the time differences between world-class times in swimming events on one hand, track and field on the other. The difference is roughly four or five to one. In the pool, it takes about 47 seconds for the best swimmers now to cover 100 meters; it's under 10 on the track. In the water, it's about 1:43 now for 200 meters, under 20 seconds on the track. The Olympic 1500-meter champion goes about 14:45 in the pool, about 3:30 on the track.

In my workouts, I was determined not only to sustain versatility but to emphasize it. I thus had to develop both speed and endurance.

An endurance block of training might last for six or seven months. I would swim nearly 50 miles each week, about 80,000 meters. Each day's workouts would come in segments, those segments based on a particular base distance (50, 100, 200 meters) as well as on the number and intensity of repetitions of the distance, the stroke, and the interval, meaning the time I'd get to rest before starting the next repetition.

The speed block could mean roughly 37 miles each week, about 60,000 meters, but with 600 to 800 meters each day at race pace.

There were times when Bob pushed me even harder.

In the winter of 2002, after the success I'd had in Fort Lauderdale, pointing toward those 2003 Worlds in Barcelona, I averaged 85,000 meters per week in the pool. The next spring, Bob ratcheted it down to 75,000. Clearly, I was going to be in outlandishly good condition.

A few years beforehand, Bob had started using another saying, one that has come to define the way he and I approach these grueling blocks of training. When we practice long and hard, he would say, we're depositing money into the bank. We need to deposit enough so that, when we make a large withdrawal, we have enough funds to do so.

In April, we went to Indianapolis for back-to-back meets, first the spring nationals, which ran over several days, the latter a one-day event called "Duel in the Pool," Americans versus Australians. At the nationals, I became the first American swimmer to win races in three different strokes: in order, the 200 back, 200 free, and 100 fly. The anticipation for the duel, intense at first, had been considerably reduced when most of the Aussies declined to take part, among them Ian. Though I wished he and the others had come, I was nevertheless on a mission; in one afternoon, I would swim four races. In the first, I lowered the world record in the 400 IM to 4:10.73; forty minutes later, I just missed the chance to become the first male swimmer to set two individual world records in a single day, finishing outside the record in the 100 fly by three-hundredths of a second; ninety minutes after that I touched out Malchow to win the 200 fly; and then, in the last race of the day, went 51.61 on the butterfly leg as we beat the Aussies in the medley relay.

I had proven to myself that I could swim multiple events against a first-rate field. In the stands, my mom held up a sign. It read: "Actions Speak Louder than Words."

Three weeks before Barcelona, we went out to California, to Santa Clara. A Finnish journalist started pestering me about whether I really thought I could break the world record in the 200 IM, 1:58.16. It had been held since 1994, nine years, by Jani Sievinen of Finland.

I told him what I typically say, that anything is possible.

"Yes," the reporter said, "but then maybe you think it is too difficult. Nobody has done this for nine years so maybe it will not happen? Why do you think you can do it?"

Here was another doubter.

I love doubters. I love all doubters. I welcome all comments.

As much as I wanted that record, however, conditions did not seem optimal. I hadn't shaved and, with Barcelona still out there, hadn't tapered. Before the race, Bob and I ran over some projected split times; those splits had me just under Sievenen's time.

I said to Bob, you're thinking I should break a world record?

He said, why not?

With each stroke, I could hear the crowd going crazy. I could tell I was swimming hard. After I finished, I saw the board and threw my hands way, way up: 1:57.94. Too difficult? Nine years? Maybe it won't happen? Why do you think you can do it?

Because I believe in myself, because I reach for my goals, and because I work to get there.

To see just what I am, truly, capable of.

Barcelona and the 2003 Worlds would be unlike anything I had ever done before. In Sydney, I had only the one race. At the 2001 Worlds in Fukuoka, I had only the one race. In Barcelona, I was looking at multiple events.

Bob, meanwhile, unearthed a story that had run in the Australian papers. The article quoted Don Talbot, the former head coach of the Australian swim team who was then a team consultant. He said I had done "nothing in the world" and still had to prove myself on the world stage.

"We know that Phelps is a good boy, but people trying to say he's a greater swimmer than Ian—absolute nonsense," Talbot said. "He has showed promise in minor meets, no pressure. When he gets under the pressure with all the great swimmers around him, and each event he gets up will be a different one, he's got to master that.

"Ian Thorpe has got all the runs on the board right now. The promise with Phelps is there, but for people saying he's going to outdo Thorpie, I live to see that day."

I read that and hoped Don was going to keep living.

Ian weighed in, too. "I think he's one of the most talented swimmers in the world," he told an Australian newspaper reporter, talking about me, "and it's obvious from his results that he has to be up there on the list of the best swimmers. But he still has a lot more things that he needs to achieve before you put him in the category of being the best."

For my part, I made sure in talking to reporters to offer nothing about Ian but praise.

"In my opinion," I said, "Ian Thorpe is the number-one swimmer in the world. People have him on a pedestal and everyone is trying to get to him.

"But we will see who is the world's number-one swimmer after the world championships."

In Barcelona, I won six medals, four gold. I became the first swimmer to break five world records at a world championship as well as the first to break world records in two individual events on the same day. I became just the third swimmer—Spitz and West Germany's Michael Gross the others—to simultaneously hold world records in four individual events, and, in our first head-to-head matchup in a world or Olympic final, I defeated Ian by nearly two body lengths in the 200 IM.

Ian, meanwhile, won the 200 free. In Barcelona, I did not take part in that race. Maybe in Athens.

At the end of the Worlds, Talbot told an Australian reporter, "Greatness comes from longevity. Michael Phelps' potential is tremendous and he may come out as the most successful at this competition. He has hit that wave and he's going.

"And if he can do it at the Olympic Games and then the next world titles, and then the next Olympic Games, he will earn the mantle of greatness."

● ● ●

That December, Ian was honored at the Australian Swimmer of the Year Awards. The Speedo $1 million incentive had just been announced a few weeks before. Naturally, Ian was asked if he thought anyone could go seven or better.

"I think it is unattainable for me and unattainable for anyone," he said.

Nothing is unattainable.

Bob and I set about trying to fix some of my technical glitches. My turns needed work, my chin had to stay down when I was swimming the fly, my breathing during the free needed to come back farther to the left. We also tried during those months to figure out which events I would swim at the Trials and thus, if all went well, at the Games. The two flys, the two IMs, three relays if the coaches would let me, all that was easy enough to figure out. But between the 200 free and the 200 back, which? Just one? Or both? Or maybe the 100 free as well?

Before the 2004 spring nationals in Orlando, Bob and I were leaning toward the 200 free. There, though, I swam the 200 back in 1:55.30. Aaron Peirsol's world record at the time was 1:55.15. That same night, I won the 100 free in 49.05.

During the spring nationals, meantime, Bob struck up a conversation with Jon Urbanchek, the University of Michigan coach who had first seen me at the pool in Baltimore when I was eleven, and who had accurately predicted when I was fifteen that I would make the Sydney Olympic team. Jon had announced in January that after twenty-two years as Michigan coach he was planning to step aside. Would Bob have any interest in the job? Curious, Bob agreed to meet with Bill Martin, the Michigan athletic director who, at the time, was also the acting president of the U.S. Olympic Committee.

Jon was widely regarded as one of the premier coaches not just in the United States but the world. A star distance swimmer for Michigan in the late 1950s and early 1960s, he spent twenty years coaching in Southern California, then returned to Ann Arbor as the Michigan coach. His teams won thirteen Big Ten championships, ten straight from 1986 to 1995; the 1995 team won the NCAA title. Jon took good swimmers and made them great: Dolan and Malchow and, before them, Mike Barrowman. And others.

The culture Jon had created in Ann Arbor, that of a demanding pursuit of excellence, was Bob's culture. Michigan, with one of the nation's most successful athletic departments, with resources vastly different than those of a club team, even a highly successful club team, could be a dream job.

The more Bob thought about it, the more, indeed, it seemed like a dream job.

Even so, he told the people at Michigan, don't hire me thinking you're going to get Michael.

Bob and I reconnected in the Bahamas, where I'd gone to shoot a commercial, swimming next to a dolphin. Relax, the crew kept saying as the dolphin would bump up against me, swim away, come back a few minutes later, and pop up again. Just don't panic. Feel free to pet her.

On the flight home to Baltimore, Bob told me the Michigan job was his. If I go there, he said, what would you do?

I knew this had to be coming one day. Here it was. I'm going with you, I said.

After Athens, Bob knew, I would have to leave Baltimore for my own personal growth. Maybe, at some level, I knew, too, hard as it would be to leave my mother and sisters. There was no way I was leaving Bob. He was my coach, yes. But he was also much, much more. A friend, yes, but still more than that. Bob had changed not only how I swam but who I was as a person, reminding me constantly how much love and dedication he has for the sport and everyone in it. I don't think either one of us, to be honest, could do without the other for any length of time. I certainly wasn't about to try.

Bob accepted the Michigan job late in March of 2004. The news broke on April 1, as we—Bob, me, some others from North Baltimore—flew to Indianapolis. As soon as we landed, reporters from all over the world—even Xinhua, the Chinese news service—knew they had a story.

Of course, in a way, this was what I was after, drawing major attention to swimming. There had been stories in the run-up to the Trials about the Olympic tattoo I had gotten on my right hip after Sydney, a cover story on *ESPN The Magazine* (as an answer to the *Sports Illustrated* swimsuit issue, I was described as "The

Hottest Thing in a Swimsuit"), a photo on the cover of David Wallechinsky's *The Complete Book of the Summer Olympics,* and more.

The crush carried on all the way through the Trials, where I qualified for the team in six individual events, including both the 200 free and the 200 back. The night of the 200 free, the finals were moved up ten minutes so that the races could air on NBC, the network's first live prime-time broadcast of the swimming Trials since it had gotten the U.S. rights to broadcast the Games way back in 1988.

Having qualified for six, how much did I want to try to take on at the Games? Once the Trials wrapped, we had all of twenty-four hours to decide; USA Swimming needed to finalize its roster. The 200 back or 200 free?

The 200 free. I wanted a shot at Ian Thorpe.

• • •

There were days, perhaps even weeks, during the seven years after the IOC awarded the 2004 Olympics to Athens, when it wasn't at all clear that Athens was going to be ready.

Athens had lobbied for the 1996 Games, the centennial anniversary of the modern Olympics, but those went to Atlanta. In 1997, as something of a makeup, the IOC gave the 2004 Games to Greece despite very real economic and political concerns.

In 2000, the IOC said preparations in Athens were coming along so slowly that it was seriously considering its options, including the possibility of moving the Games somewhere else. Six months before the Games, the main Olympic park, which was called OAKA, remained a dusty construction zone. The Olympic pool, inside the OAKA zone, was going to go without a roof, officials finally announced. If it was hot and humid during the competitions, well, it was, after all, a pool.

Mostly, even before 2001, the buzz had to do over and again

with security concerns. A radical anarchists' group called 17 November, who had assassinated U.S. officials and influential Greeks, had been on the loose for years. Then, of course, came 9/11. Osama bin Laden declared holy war on everything American. The IOC took out insurance against terrorism and other disasters. In the months before the Olympics, most American reporters who were going to be sent to Athens had to go through disaster training taught, in many cases, by former military specialists; the training was heavy on such notions as how to bandage up a wounded arm or leg in case a bomb went off. This was the atmosphere heading into Athens and, for those of us on the American team, there were additional concerns, which the U.S. Olympic Committee made clear in instructing us to be as low-key as possible. We were to avoid at all costs anything that might paint any one of us as ugly Americans.

I certainly wasn't going to do anything stupid. And I certainly felt secure.

"I feel extremely safe, extremely confident," I said in meeting reporters before the Olympics started. "The USA is doing a great job of supporting us and protecting us, especially the swim team. We wear the red, white, and blue proudly. We wear the stars and stripes."

I certainly was not going to comment on anything political. I understood that I was now a public figure, and that there might be interest in my take on such things, if I had one. That said, I was nineteen years old, a swimmer focused on swimming.

"Bush or Kerry?" I was asked at a pre-Olympics U.S. swim team training camp in Mallorca, Spain. Who did I prefer in the 2004 U.S. presidential election?

"The objective at hand is swimming," I said. "That's what I'm worried about right now."

The sooner the attention shifted to sports, and to swimming, the better.

As it usually does at the Olympics, it did so as soon as the action got under way at that outdoor pool, enveloped by bleachers that slanted up and away into the sky, decorated by flags from countries near and far that fluttered in the breeze.

The 400 IM took place on a Saturday, the 400 free relay Sunday, the 200 free Monday.

Heading into that 200 free in Athens, then, I was one-for-two. The Spitz Watch was at full roar for what was being called the "Race of the Century," which seemed absurd given that the century's years could still be counted on one hand.

At these Olympics, Bob was one of Eddie Reese's three assistants. Entertaining the press before the 200 free, Bob was asked to equate it with a horse race. He brought up the 1938 classic when Seabiscuit challenged War Admiral. But this was not a match race, he emphasized.

Indeed not.

The first semifinal went to van den Hoogenband. Ian and I went one-two in the other.

Klete Keller was also in the race; he finished second behind me at the Trials and had just two days before won his second straight Olympic bronze in the 400. Hackett was in, too; he'd held the world record in the 200 free for a few months in 1999.

Why, I kept getting asked, did I want into this race?

It's not your best event, I kept getting told. It's the one race in which you're not the favorite. Ian is the world-record holder, Hoogie the defending Olympic champion. Don't you get that?

I heard the murmurs: If you lose this race, it's over; you can't win seven golds at these Olympics.

Don't you understand?

Yes, I understood fully. I wanted to race in this race, against the guys who made up this field. And I especially wanted to race Ian Thorpe, the world-record holder, before either of us was done.

The point of competition is to compete. It's to take on the biggest challenge. When you compete against the very best, it

The little boy who would grow to become the greatest gold medalist in Olympic history turns three with a backyard birthday party.

What a future Olympic gold medalist looks like on his first day of kindergarten: Michael boarding the school bus under the watch of big sister Whitney.

Michael at eight with Hilary (left) and Whitney, the sisters
in Christmas pajamas, a Phelps family tradition.

Back problems kept Whitney (left)
from achieving her Olympic goals,
adding incentive for a teenage Michael
to carry forward the family dream.

Michael at fifteen warming up before the 200 fly at the 2000 U.S. Trials, the meet that would send him to his first Summer Olympics.

At the 2001 world championships, sixteen-year-old Michael (right) takes gold in the 200 fly; Tom Malchow, Olympic champion only the year before in Sydney, claims silver.

Michael taking off at the Pan Pacific swim championships in 2006 in the 200 backstroke, an event he hasn't tried to race at the Olympics—yet.

Michael not only wins this 200 fly in Texas in 2001 but, timed in 1:54.92, makes swim history as the youngest world-record holder—fifteen years, nine months.

Not just great theater, but a gesture of genuine solidarity and support
at the 2004 Olympic Trials from the one and only Mark Spitz (left),
winner of seven gold medals at the 1972 Munich Games.

A beaming Michael just a few
minutes after out-touching Ian
Crocker by four-hundredths
of a second to win gold in the
100 butterfly at the 2004
Athens Olympics.

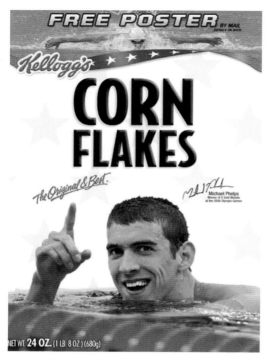

What could be more all-American? After the 2008 Olympics, Michael appears on special boxes of Kellogg's Corn Flakes and Frosted Flakes.

They're off in the race that rocked the 2007 worlds in Melbourne. Michael, fifth from bottom, is en route to a stunning 1:43.86 in the 200 free, breaking Ian Thorpe's world record by two-tenths of a second.

Seeing clearly in the prelims of the 100 fly in Beijing—in goggles borrowed from teammate Ricky Berens—after a nearly disastrous goggles malfunction the day before in the 200 fly final.

Anchored by coach Bob Bowman (center) the high-performance Club Wolverine training crew—Michael at the far right—a few months before the Beijing Games.

Michael tuning in before turning it on in the 200 individual medley final in Beijing, his sixth gold. His 2008 Games iPod favorites: Lil Wayne, Young Jeezy.

The beauty and grace of swimming at its highest levels as so elegantly revealed underwater: Michael (center) in the heats of the 200 fly at the Water Cube in Beijing.

His butterfly a study in power and fluidity, Michael helps lift the United States to a gold medal and a world record in the medley relay at the 2008 Olympics.

A furious comeback capped by a chopped half-stroke at the wall leads to elation in the 100 butterfly in Beijing: victory for Michael by one-hundredth of a second, his seventh 2008 Games gold.

The defining image of victory in Beijing: Garrett Weber-Gale (left) and Michael as the United States, with Jason Lezak anchoring, defeats the French in the 400 freestyle relay.

Tearfully, joyfully amazed in the stands: mom Debbie Phelps (left) and oldest sister Hilary after Michael wins his eighth gold medal in Beijing.

Huddling up on deck after the stirring 400 free relay victory in Beijing: Garrett Weber-Gale, Jason Lezak, Michael, Cullen Jones.

Michael, enveloped by clamoring photographers, finds his mother and sisters after his final race, the medley relay, at the 2008 Beijing Games.

Honoring America in victory: teammates Brendan Hansen (left) and Jason Lezak (right) flanking Michael after the 2008 Beijing Games medley relay.

Stillness before the storm: The scene inside the Water Cube, Beijing's Olympic swimming and diving venue, before competition at the 2008 Games gets underway.

Eight gold medals,
fifth *Sports Illustrated* cover
shot—what *SI* jinx?

A loving son and brother: Michael shares a quiet moment backstage
in Beijing with his mom, Debbie, and sisters Whitney (left) and Hilary.

After the 2008 Games and years of dedication and sacrifice, it was time
for a little fun: Michael unwinding at Disney's Epcot Center on a Segway scooter.

There was no time during the 2008 Games to tour
the Forbidden City or other Beijing landmarks.
That came the year before with the likes of Katie Hoff,
another Baltimore swim star.

A familiar scene for Michael in the weeks after the 2008 Games, being asked by appreciative fans for an autograph or a photo, here outside the *Today* show set in New York.

In the aftermath of the eight Olympic medals that he won at the Athens Games, six gold, Michael savors the thrill of being an honorary captain for his favorite NFL team, the Baltimore Ravens, in a 2004 victory over the Cleveland Browns.

"Phelpstival" is what they called the celebration in Maryland after the 2004 Athens Games, officials naming the street next to Towson High School "Michael Phelps Way."

One of Michael's ultimate goals is getting more young people into swimming, as he does here with these kids in New York after the 2008 Games.

makes you better; I don't care if someone is twenty times better, or one-tenth better. I want to race the best.

I hate to lose. But I was not afraid to lose. I am never afraid to lose.

There's a dry wind that's peculiar to Greece that's called the *meltemi*. It comes up in the late afternoons and early evenings. As we were called out onto the deck, the flags around the stadium were blowing straight out because of the *meltemi*.

I was in Lane 3, Hoogie in 4, Ian in 5.

There were cheers for me when I was introduced. There were more cheers for Hoogie. The cheers for Ian were deafening.

At the 50 wall, I was in fourth. No surprise there. Hoogie was under world-record pace. By the 100 wall, I had moved into third. We stayed in that order through the third wall: Hoogie, Ian, me. At the 150 wall, though, Ian came off the turn like a rocket. He overtook Hoogie and drove to the finish. I came on hard and, over that last 50, threw down the fastest last split in the pool. I made up more than a second on Hoogie, and touched in 1:45.32, an American record and a time that would have won gold at every prior Olympic Games, even in Sydney just four years before.

Here it was good for third. I was still third.

Hoogie touched nine-hundredths ahead of me, in 1:45.23. He got second.

Ian was first, in 1:44.71, an Olympic record. As he touched, he ripped off his yellow cap, squinted at the board, saw the number "1" next to his name, pumped his right fist and yelled, "Yeah! Whoo!" He and Hoogie exchanged a handshake over the lane line, and a hug, and Ian, leaning in so Pieter could hear over the crowd noise, said, "Well, I guess that makes it one-all and I'd like to see you again in Beijing."

Later, talking to the press, Hoogie said, "I gave my best but Thorpe was better. He is the man in this distance. To be beaten by one of the best in my sport, well, that's the way it is."

Ian said, "You know, people kind of have their fate and their destiny and, you know, that was what it was tonight. I've worked damn hard for this. I've worked hard for all of my swims and, you know, it just happened for me tonight."

"Just the fact that Phelps wanted to step up and race Ian Thorpe, even though this isn't his best event, it's a testament to what kind of athlete he is," one of the television commentators said just moments after the finish. The commentator: Dara Torres, who was taking part in these Olympics from the broadcasting booth.

That effort in Athens was, at the time, the fastest I could go. I had made mistakes: My turns could have been so much better, particularly my third turn, which just killed me. Even so, I was closing fast and if the race had been 205 or 210 meters, I might have pulled it out. But it wasn't, of course, and so I didn't. I ran out of pool; that's the saying in swimming, and that's what happened.

But, I can see now, it's all part of how the puzzle was supposed to come together.

That loss in Athens has to be looked at as a—maybe *the*—defining moment in my swim career. I stepped up and raced the best. I found out I was good but, in the 200 free, not good enough. I had work to do. I was proud to stand on the podium with Pieter and Ian, with Ian in particular—it's competitive, never personal—but at the same time I felt immense resolve.

During the ceremony, as the gold medal was draped around his neck, I applauded in genuine respect, and I made sure afterward, in speaking with reporters, to praise him. "In my opinion, he has a perfect stroke," I said. "It's unbelievable how he moves through the water. It's pretty to watch."

He, in turn, said nice things about me: "Michael had a good race." But he also said, when asked, that seven golds might be too much for anyone. "It is a very difficult thing to do. I think people probably don't understand what goes on behind the scenes."

Spitz Watch was over, at least for 2004. I had tried to do something bold. I didn't quite get there, at least in Athens. But isn't the trying the thing that matters? I was taught to dream big. If you don't, don't you fall back?

When I was told, well after the Games, what was being said about me then, after I had won one gold medal and two bronzes, it was fascinating to learn that in some quarters I could be seen as a disappointment.

"Although Phelps could still win six gold medals in Athens," the Associated Press reported, "his audacious challenge fell short and could result in him being remembered as something of a failure at the Athens Games . . ."

I knew I was not a failure in any way, and so did those close to me. It doesn't matter if you fall short; it is never a failure to go after your goals with everything you've got. "'Will it crush him?' 'No,'" my mom said in that same AP story. "'He's already got a page in the history book.'"

• • •

To anyone who would listen in 2004, Bob would say, remember, Michael is only nineteen. We don't know how good he is yet. We're going to try to do whatever we can to get him to deliver his best performances. That's all I can do and that's all he can do.

After the 200 free in Athens, I could still win eight medals at those 2004 Games but only five more golds, which, as it turned out, I did. When those Olympics were over, I had become the second athlete in Olympic history to win eight total medals at a single Games; a gymnast from the Soviet Union, Alexander Ditiatin, won eight at the 1980 Games in Moscow.

That was immensely gratifying, of course. People would ask me, is it a disappointment not to win seven golds? I would say, I won eight medals, how is that a disappointment?

At the same time, I had a new measuring stick: that 200 free. I didn't yet know how good I could be. There was obviously more to do to get me to deliver my best. Between Athens and Beijing, as Bob and I mapped out the plan to get to 2008, we had three major meets that would test how far I could come: the 2005 world championships in Montreal; the 2006 Pan Pacs, again in Canada, this time out west, in Victoria; and the 2007 world championships in Melbourne.

I fully expected to get better. After Athens, as I grew into my twenties, I was bound to get bigger and stronger. In Ann Arbor, Bob could call on Jon's expertise as well; though Jon was formally stepping aside as Michigan's head coach, he was still going to be very much around. Jon knew a few things about how to get the world's best swimmers ready for the biggest meets, including the Olympics, where he had been an assistant coach at multiple editions of the Games.

Both Ian and Hoogie passed on the 2005 Worlds in Montreal, Ian saying he was taking the year off, Pieter recovering from back surgery. I won the 200 free there in 1:45.20, a personal best and a tenth of a second lower than the American record I had set in Athens. Hackett finished second, nearly a second behind. Halfway through the race, I was steaming along, ahead of Ian's world-record pace. But my last turn was still off. And then it was obvious, coming down the last 50, I was not in the most optimal condition. It was clear to Bob, and to me, that I had taken a major withdrawal from the account in Athens, and now needed to make significant deposits.

The most puzzling thing about that 200 final in Montreal is that it came two days after a disastrous 400 free prelim; I finished eighteenth of fifty-seven swimmers, and failed for the first time in years to advance to the final. In my 400 prelim, I had been third in my heat at the turn, then faded to seventh. Looking at the scoreboard, I couldn't believe it. I still can't. I am at a loss to explain why it happened. It just did.

It was a lesson I would rather not have been reminded of, that racing at a world-class level takes everything you've got, and you have to bring it each and every day. But I got reminded. I would be reminded of that time and again in Montreal, particularly later in that meet, in the 100 fly.

Every day thereafter, at the pool or in the weight room in Ann Arbor, I felt the sting. My response to that, the work that losing would spur me to put in, that was something I could control. Ian Thorpe's willingness to keep swimming: that I had no control over.

The work I was putting in jumped to a new level. Everything I accomplished in the pool leading up to and through Athens had been done without my doing any serious weightlifting. When I was growing, Bob had been particularly worried that weight work might do more harm than good, might well lead to serious injury. There was good reason for that, I am double-jointed in my knees, my ankles, and my elbows. I was, especially as a teenager, awkward out of the pool. Clumsy, even. Bob finally ordered me to stop jogging because I couldn't even do that without running the risk of tripping over my own feet.

After 2005, both of us understood the time had come. Yes, I had speed in the pool, but that was mostly because I could hold a steady pace over whatever distance was demanded. Now, I needed to build more sprint speed. One sure way would be producing ferocious drive off the wall in my turns. To do that, my legs needed to get much stronger.

I went from having never lifted so much as a barbell in my life to grueling workouts in the weight room three days a week, the weight work typically following two hours in the pool.

Because so much of the motion that's visible in the pool is with the arms, it's easy for most people in the stands or watching on television to think that swimming is all about the arms. Olympic swimming, like all long-course racing, is all in the legs.

Eight Olympic medals, six gold, and, when I started doing the box squat at Michigan, one of the most basic of strength-building exercises for the legs, I was lucky to be able to max out one rep at 300 pounds. I worked up to twenty.

To my disappointment, Ian did not show in Victoria, at the 2006 Pan Pacs. Word was he was living in Los Angeles. It was unclear to some whether swimming still motivated him.

With Ian out, I opted in Victoria not to swim the 200 free, pouring myself instead into the 200 fly (world record); that 400 relay with Neil, Cullen, and Jason (world record); and the 200 IM (world record). After no such records for almost two years, I suddenly had three.

The Pan Pacs were in August. That fall, I was at the condo I'd bought in Ann Arbor, just hanging around amid practices, messing around on the computer, and watching television, when I got a text message from a friend. It said, "Thorpe just retired." My first reaction was, no way. My second was, no way that could be true.

It was true.

Ian held a news conference in Sydney to say he simply was no longer motivated to keep swimming.

He had won eleven world titles, set thirteen long-course world records, and won five Olympic gold medals. And, just like that, it was over. He had never really gotten back into the pool after Athens and now he never would.

We issued a statement in which I called Ian "an inspiration and a terrific champion." The statement said Ian had "elevated the worldwide interest in swimming and was a great ambassador to our sport." It also said, because this was indisputably the right thing to do, "I wish him the best of luck in the future."

Which I wholeheartedly did. Even as I wished he were still swimming.

It took a while to sink in: I was never going to get the chance, ever again, to race him like we raced in Athens.

Just once more with the Aussie in the full-length black bodysuit, the man I considered the world's greatest freestyler. That's what I wanted. Head-to-head, he and I, to see what would happen now if he were at his best and me at mine.

A couple months before the 2007 worlds, I went to Bob and asked him for video of all my swims from Athens. He didn't push this on me; this was me asking. I took those videos and watched them over and over. When I watched the 200 free from the 2004 Olympics, I understood clearly that I had gone out too slowly and that the third turn had left me at an impossible disadvantage. It was abundantly clear what I needed to fix. In Melbourne, I would have to swim the race aggressively from the start. Power through the turns, especially the third. The big mistake I could make would be to let van den Hoogenband get ahead early, then have to reel him in, the way I'd tried to do in Athens, when he and Ian went out ahead.

At least I'd have the satisfaction of racing Hoogie, even if Ian was not going to be in this race.

And then Don Talbot opened his mouth. Again.

"Thorpe is still number one in my opinion, and Phelps doesn't outdo him yet," Talbot was quoted in Australian newspapers a few days before the meet got underway.

There was more: ". . . The Americans want to claim they invented Jesus Christ before he came, and the same thing with Phelps—they were saying he was the greatest in the world when Thorpey was the thing.

"I said he was a great swimmer but he's not there yet and they got into me about it . . . Certainly he's on the right track. If he wins at this meet what he's planning to do, then there is no doubt he'll be the best male swimmer of all time. He will supersede Thorpe.

". . . He doesn't want to be one of the greatest, he wants to be the greatest, and regardless of what I think, I think he has to outdo Spitz next year at the Olympics. Whether he can do that, I don't know."

I said nothing.

The day of the 200 free final, dipping into the warm-up pool, I felt it. My freestyle had never, ever felt that smooth. Right then and there, I thought, something special might happen here. Something really special.

No time on the books was even within a half-second of Ian's world-record 1:44.06, the swim from Fukuoka in 2001. The only other person to even break 1:45 had been van den Hoogenband.

Hoogie lined up for the finals in Melbourne in Lane 4; he'd had the fastest semifinal swim. I drew Lane 5. I turned first at the first wall, at 24.47, and again at the second, at 51-flat. Hoogie seemed to still be there with me, just off my shoulder, but, as I had planned, I was ahead. That third leg, I opened it up a bit, and after I turned and finally surfaced, I could hear the crowd noise getting louder and louder. The big video board in Melbourne was showing the race and, through a superimposed red line, it was also showing where I was in relationship to world-record pace. Obviously I was ahead, or at least close. In the water, I had no idea how far ahead. I just knew I had lost sight of Hoogie.

That last lap, Bob would say later, was perhaps the best lap he had ever seen. At least at the time. He knew the race was over at 50 meters, when I'd beaten everyone to that first wall. He had turned to Mark Schubert, the U.S. national coach, and said, this one's done. Mark would say later it looked like I was racing Ian even though Ian wasn't in the pool.

Bob had been hoping for 1:44-something.

I touched, turned, and looked at the clock. It read 1:43.86.

Not just a world record. A world record by two-tenths of a second. And better than I had ever done before in the 200 free by nearly a second and a half. I had erased Thorpe's name from the record books, in his own country.

I was so far ahead that I had time not only to touch but to spin to see the board, jam my left index finger into the air and grab the lane rope with my right arm before Hoogie, in the next lane over, touched the wall. He then turned, saw the board, which said that he was more than two seconds behind at 1:46.28, and came over to the lane line to exchange a handshake.

By then, I'd even had time to duck down, drink water, and spray some around in front of me. I have no idea why I do this. Just a quirk after big races.

Hoogie said to me, "Where did that come from?"

I answered honestly. "I don't know."

"What was your best time before that?"

"1:45.2."

"Off every wall," he said, "the only thing I could look at was your underwaters. I couldn't focus on any part of my race." And then he said, "I won't swim that next year," meaning in Beijing.

•　　•　　•

Ian arrived in Beijing on the eve of the Games, declared he admired my tenacity, and called me one of the greatest athletes in the world. And: "I have said before that I don't think he can do the eight, and still believe that. Mind you, if there is any person on the planet who is capable, it is him. It's sad, but I just don't think it will happen."

I said nothing.

Hoogie had been good to his word. He did not compete in the 200 free in Beijing. That meant the two swimmers most likely to chase after me were Peter Vanderkaay, one of my training partners in Ann Arbor, and Park Tae-Hwan of South Korea. Park was an excellent closer who, by the day of the 200 free final, had already won the 400 free; Peter hails from a family of top-notch University of Michigan swimmers and had, predictably, gotten even better under Bob and Jon's direction. He also was the centerpiece of what became one of Bob's favorite stories. Bob named a horse after the Vanderkaay family. The Vanderkaays instead of me?

Well, Bob would say, first of all that's a lot of pressure to put on a horse. Second, and here came the punch line, this horse is too nice.

The one that bites, he said, that one I'll name Michael.

The 200 free prelims went down the night of the 400 IM final; the semifinals the morning of the 400 relay finals. I went an easy 1:46.48 in the prelims, 1:46.28 in the semis. I didn't care what time I got in the semifinal, really, as long as it got me a lane in the finals. The way the schedule worked, I had to swim the 200 semi at 10:13 Monday morning; the relay final took place just 71 minutes later. That Monday night, I swam in the prelims of the 200 fly.

The 200 free final, then, was the seventh of what was planned to be seventeen swims. Heading out to the deck, walking to Lane 6, where my semifinal time had placed me, I was already more than a third of the way done.

I was more than satisfied to be in Lane 6. It was not important to come in first in the preliminary or semifinal heats. If those times were, for me, ordinary, no worries, at least not on my part. Those were races to get into the final, that's all.

On my goal sheet, after that 1:43.86 in Melbourne, I had put down 1:43.5 as my target for 2008 and Beijing.

That turned out to be conservative. I felt good on the blocks that Tuesday morning. Very good.

I had thought the 200 free in Melbourne was pretty close to perfect.

This one: better.

The plan, as it was in Melbourne, was to go all out. No easy speed in the front half. Hard speed. Take it out and, in essence, dare the others to catch me. I wanted to be at 100 meters in a fraction over 50 seconds. Not 51. 50 point-something.

Immediately after the beep, I surged to the lead. When I popped up after the first turn, I could see I was already half a body length ahead. By the second of the four laps, I could tell I was way out in front. Studying the stat sheets later, I saw I hit the 100 wall in 50.29.

In this race, the weight work I'd done really showed. I had more endurance. I could hold a stronger kick longer. The dolphin kick had become more or less a fifth stroke. I now had developed incredible power off the turns and, in particular, that third turn. What once had been a vulnerability was now a killer asset, 12 or 13 meters underwater, enough to help reshape the contours of what was possible in the 200 free.

I hit that third turn in 1:16.84, almost two full seconds ahead of Peter.

I drove home. Four years before, in the Race of the Century, I was third, the one individual race in Athens I did not win. Now, in Beijing, untold hours of work in the pool and weight room later, I was going to take first.

In world-record time: 1:42.96.

Park finished second, in 1:44.85; Peter got bronze, in 1:45.14. Park had indeed closed fast, 26.17 over the final 50; I had gone even faster, 26.12.

"Phelps swims so fast," Park would say later. "It is my honor to compete with him."

A roar of applause and sound washed over me. My left elbow resting on the deck, I raised my right arm and pointed up, a number-one sign, a tribute to everyone who had helped me get to that moment.

This was history.

Indeed, so much history was made at the instant I touched that last wall in the 200 free.

Park finished 1.89 seconds behind me. That was by far the biggest margin of victory in an Olympic 200 free. West Germany's Gross had won by 1.66 seconds in 1984.

In 1972, the 200 free was the race after which Spitz had exuberantly raised his shoes. Four years later, in Montreal, Bruce Furniss, John Naber, and Jim Montgomery went one-two-three in the

200 free; I had become the first American since then to win the event.

And, of course, I was three-for-three in Beijing; this third gold was the ninth of my Olympic career. I had just tied four legends of the Olympics: Spitz; another American, track star Carl Lewis; Paavo Nurmi of Finland, a distance-running star; and Larissa Latynina, a Soviet gymnast. Each of them had won nine Olympics golds.

I am honored to be in their company. To be listed in the same sentence is just incredible.

At the time, though, I didn't have time to contemplate history. Looking at the clock, I knew I was barely going to have time to get ready for the semifinals of the 200 fly, which would start in forty-six minutes from the instant I had made that number-one sign. That's mostly what I was thinking about. The 200 fly semis would be my eighth race of seventeen. None of the rest of it mattered, none of it would matter, unless I kept my focus on what was immediately at hand.

I warmed down for as many minutes as I could. I changed into my red, white, and blue warm-up gear for the medal ceremony. On my way back to the backstage pool, intending to sneak in just a few minutes of warm-up for the 200 fly semis, my mind already thinking ahead to that race, seeing the ready room, the blocks, the dive into the water, I stopped for just a moment to reach into the stands and give the flowers presented to medal winners to my sister Hilary.

As I started to hustle off, she reached her hands up to her face. And wiped away tears.

4

DETERMINATION:
THE 200 FLY

One thing that separates Michael from other swimmers, Bob likes to say, is that if they don't feel good they don't swim good.

That's not the way it is for Michael.

Michael, he says, performs no matter how he's feeling. He has practiced it a long time. He knows exactly what he wants to get done, and he's able to compartmentalize what's important.

Bob, with his seemingly endless collection of sayings, naturally has an acronym to describe the mental aspect to my racing. It's "W.I.N.: What's Important Now?"

It's true. When it comes down to it, when the time comes to focus and be mentally prepared, I can do whatever it takes to get there, in any situation.

I can because I know this, too: At the highest level of sports, and especially at the Olympics, you have to expect that everyone competing against you has physical talent. So: How do you channel peak performance into championship performance? You have to be mentally tough, that's how.

How do you get to be mentally tough? You have to train your mind just like you train the body.

Unleash your imagination. Work hard. Embrace obstacles, difficulties, and mistakes.

Nothing in life is easy. You can't wake up one day, announce you're going to go do something, and expect it to be a success. At least not consistently. You have to put time and energy and whatever you've got into it. You have to want to do it, want it badly.

That's the point that perhaps some people who say they want something, whatever that something is, don't fully understand. A lot of swimmers I trained with said they wanted to achieve something great but didn't truly put time, energy, dedication, and heart into it.

I put time, energy, dedication, heart, and soul into it.

If I wasn't in the right mood to practice, I got myself into that right mood. I'm not saying that Bob and I didn't disagree, even argue with each other—of course we did—but I got myself into the place I needed to be to get the work done that I needed to get done.

When you're challenged: What's important now?

When it gets to be race day: What's important right now?

And when things don't go right on race day, and you absolutely have to take action: What's important this very instant? Sometimes there simply is no time to think. The situation demands action: What's it going to be?

As I lined up on the blocks for the finals of the 200 fly on Wednesday morning, the 13th of August, the first of two finals I would swim that morning—the second would be the leadoff leg of the 800 freestyle relay not even an hour later—I could not have been more ready to rock. The 200 fly was my race. This was the event in which I had first set a world record seven years before.

Thousands of miles away in Norway, Fernando Canales, an

assistant Michigan swimming coach, and his wife, Mona Nyheim-Canales, were watching on television. Fernando is a former All-American swimmer at Michigan who represented his native Puerto Rico in three Olympics; Mona is a Norwegian swim champ, a swim coach in her own right, and a sports psychologist with an incredible eye for detail.

The television camera zoomed in on me during introductions. Watching in Norway, Mona turned to Fernando. She said, you know what? His cap and goggles look really weird.

●　　●　　●

The back problems I had after Athens, the broken bone in 2005, and the broken wrist in 2007 were just some of the obstacles that had confronted me, and that I had to overcome, if I were to reach my goals at the 2008 Olympics.

Everyone has obstacles to overcome.

I learned that early in life.

But I also learned another essential truth early. Dedication, grit, and willpower could go a long way in meeting, and beating, whatever challenges I would face.

As a very little boy, I was not just always on the go; I simply could not sit still. I would twirl pens and pencils between my fingers. I made faces at cameras. I climbed on everything. I never shut up. Never. I had a question for everything, and wouldn't stop asking questions until I got the answer. If then. My energy level, my talkative nature, my restlessness; all this came as a complete surprise to a mother with two girls. Mom's girlfriends who were the mothers of boys would tell her all these stories about these young boys and she'd be confounded. "My girls don't do that," she would say.

And then I came along.

The baby brother in a house full of strong women. Even as little girls, Hilary and Whitney had dynamic personalities. Of course. They took after their mother.

Early in my elementary school years, my mom kept getting phone calls about what was routinely described as my "negative" behavior.

"Michael is not paying attention in class."

"Michael is having difficulty focusing in class."

"Michael is not doing his work the way he needs to be doing his work."

"Michael always hurries."

"Michael is agitating other children in the class."

Finally, my mom and the teacher held a meeting.

"Michael just can't focus," the teacher said.

"Well," Mom said, "maybe it's because Michael is bored with what he's being taught."

"Mrs. Phelps, are you saying that Michael is gifted? Michael is not gifted," the teacher said.

I was just seven when my parents split up. I didn't understand.

I had big ears. I was scrawny. I got picked on, a lot. Still in elementary school, I had a Mickey Mouse baseball hat. One day I got on the bus with the hat. I got off the bus without it. A bunch of older kids would pick on me and throw my hat around; one of them threw the hat out the window.

Another encounter: I was about eleven or twelve. We were at a swim meet. The older boys were about to dump my head in the toilet, give me a swirlie, as it was called, until someone came in, maybe Bob, maybe another group of kids, I don't remember, and I escaped. I do remember this: I ran out of that bathroom in tears.

My anger would build up inside and, while I wouldn't say anything about it to anyone, I would use that anger as motivation, especially at the pool.

At a swim meet in Princeton, New Jersey, a kid from Delaware beat me in a 200-yard freestyle race. This would have been just the sort of thing that typically would have sparked a first-class, goggles-throwing tantrum. Instead, I felt the burn inside, then let the emotion carry me through my next swims. At that meet, I had five more events. I won all five.

Looking back, I firmly believe these episodes taught me not just how to manage my emotions to my advantage. I also learned what was worth getting worked up about, what was meaningful and important in my life. And, it follows naturally, what was not.

I also saw firsthand, watching my mother, what family values and work ethic truly meant.

When I was in sixth grade, our family physician, Dr. Charles Wax, diagnosed me with attention deficit/hyperactivity disorder. ADHD is a relatively common childhood disorder; it can make it difficult for a child to do well in school or behave at home. The doctor prescribed the stimulant Ritalin.

Initially, the Ritalin program was three times a day during the school week: morning, lunchtime, dinner. I did not take Ritalin on weekends. Staying busy with sports, increasingly swimming, would burn off my energy. At school, the lunchtime dose meant I had to go to the school nurse's office. If I didn't remember, the nurse would come call me out of my next class. For a kid who was already being picked on, this was another reason to stand out. Why was the nurse coming to get me? Where was I going with the nurse all the time? What was going on?

Mom did not tell me at first what Ritalin was or what it was supposed to do. In class, I noticed I did seem less jumpy.

For her part, my mother, raising three kids by herself, pursuing her own career goals, just worked harder to make sure I was, indeed, not only focusing in class but was doing my homework.

So many times, it seemed, I would do my homework and bring it to her for a review, and she'd say, "Michael, your handwriting is so small, I can't read this." She'd rip it up, then and there.

"Mom!"

"You can't read this, Michael. You need to go back and do this again. And it has to be legible."

Doing it until I learned to do it right was one of my mom's many important lessons.

As I got into middle school, another teacher told mom in one of those parent-teacher conferences that I would never be successful at anything I did because I couldn't concentrate.

"So," my mom told this teacher right back, "what are you doing about it?"

At home, this was what she and I were doing about it. Okay, my mom would say, what's your topic?

I'd say, the Louisiana Purchase, or whatever it was, and she would say, okay, give me four main facts about your topic that you want to say.

I'd do that, and she'd say, great, now tell me about the first of those four points. It happened in 1803, I might say. And then the second. Lewis and Clark were assigned to explore the territory. And so on, until she had helped me work my way through the entire assignment.

There was no slacking off just because it might be difficult or because I didn't want to do it. I was expected to do the right thing.

Which is why, in seventh grade, I went to my mom and said, I wanted to stop taking Ritalin.

She said, "Are you sure?"

And, "How do you think you're going to be able to control yourself in the classroom?"

"Do you think you can get through your schoolwork without it?"

"Will you be able to accomplish everything you want to accomplish without the Ritalin?"

"Do you think you can get through not just your academics but manage your swim schedule, too?"

Yes, I said. I don't know if it was that I didn't want to go to the nurse's office, or that I thought I had beaten it. But I knew I didn't want to take Ritalin anymore. I viewed it as an unnecessary crutch. I was mentally tough enough to go without it, I was sure.

Okay, she said, Let's try it. Let's go talk to Dr. Wax, but let's not go cold turkey.

The doctor gradually weaned me off the medicine. The first to be cut out was that lunchtime dose. In short order, the frequency of the other doses was reduced, then eliminated entirely.

This was big. And not just because I was off the medicine. I had proven to myself that I could set a goal and, through willpower and being mentally tough, not only meet that goal but beat it.

And so: If I dedicated myself to my goals, if I worked as hard as I could—I could accomplish anything.

• • •

It was Dr. Wax who had suggested years before that Hilary and Whitney learn to swim. Every child should be water safe, he said.

Hilary turned out to be a very good swimmer. She set three school records at the University of Richmond.

Whitney turned out to be a very, very good swimmer, even though, a lot like me, she didn't want to get in the water at first. She had to be bribed with a Snickers bar. Once she got in, though, she didn't want to get out. And once she started to get better, she got really, really good. From 1990 to 1993, she was named Maryland's outstanding swimmer. The next year, when she was just thirteen, she finished second in the 200 fly at the spring nationals; that earned her a spot on her first world championship team. She went to Rome—she was fourteen by then—and finished ninth, and came back with all kinds of stories about being there. And a bunch of free stuff.

It was impossible not to hear the buzz: Whitney would be the next great American swim star. The gold medals were all but hers.

Of course everyone we knew was getting excited. The Christmas before those 1996 Games, an uncle, my mom's brother, B.J., gave Whitney a 1996 Atlanta mug. She said, I'm going to be there!

Whitney loved the routine, the discipline, the challenge of swimming. Up before dawn. If a coach told her to do ten laps, she would do twelve. If there was a blizzard and it wasn't safe to drive to practice, on went the parka and the boots, because it was time to walk there.

The pool was Whitney's passion, her outlet, her comfort. Even now, with a husband, two small children, and a job, she goes to the gym at five in the morning because it is what she has always done and is still a major part of who she is.

When Whitney was ten or eleven, her back started hurting. Halfway through her swim practices, her back would start feeling sore.

Whitney is not a quitter. She kept at it.

At thirteen, her back would hurt each time she'd do a flip turn. Her arms and legs would tingle. One day after practice, she bent down in the kitchen to pick up some fruit. She couldn't get back up.

Eventually, she did get back up, and at practice kept pushing through the stabbing pain. She was swimming in an elite NBAC group, seven girls, and the unspoken rule was: You don't get out.

Whitney is not the sort to show her emotions. For her to cry, she's got to be really hurting. She would swim through many a practice crying during the sets. No one knew because, after all, she was in a pool. Later, she would find out that two of the discs in her lower back had herniated; another disc in her neck was bulging.

If she couldn't actually gut out the swimming itself, Whitney still showed up at the pool. While the other girls were doing their sets, Whitney would hang in an outside lane, jogging in the water. She was not going to miss practice.

At the same time Whitney was confronted with all this back

pain, she was also wrestling with food-related issues. She was already doing all she could in the pool. Was there something else she could to make herself go faster? Lose weight, she thought. If she were skinnier, she'd have to go faster, right?

Whitney stopped eating snacks. Then she began to eat less at meals. Mom noticed and, every now and then, asked Whitney about it. Nothing's wrong, Mom, Whitney would say. Mom took Whitney to a nutritionist, who instructed her to keep a food diary and to post that diary on our mom's door. The entries went up; Whitney may or may not have been eating what she had written down she had eaten. The nutritionist gave our mother tips like this: Put butter in Whitney's potatoes. Whitney was too clever for that. She would come home from these grueling swim practices and do sit-ups in front of the TV.

Not surprisingly, Whitney's training began to suffer. After long sessions in the water, she would turn blue. She got good at staying under the water until her color came back.

Whitney came into the 1996 Trials, held in Indianapolis, with the best time in the nation in the 200 fly, 2:11.04. She finished sixth.

I knew nothing of any of Whitney's eating-related issues or her back problems. All I knew that day in Indianapolis was that Hilary and Mom were in tears after the race.

Several months after the Trials, Whitney confided that her back pain was worse than she had let on. She also sought help for her eating habits.

I saw her overcome all of that.

Then I saw her overcome her own heartache.

Before the Trials, college swim coaches were keenly interested in Whitney. Afterward, she was suddenly without that attention. She finally did get an offer, from the University of Nevada at Las Vegas. After time away from the pool, she came back, won her conference title, was named the conference's "newcomer of the year," and made the cut for the 2000 Trials. That spring, she came home and started training again at NBAC. But it didn't take long for her back to start hurting again. Rather than enter a race she knew she'd have no chance at winning and jeopardize her health over the long term, she withdrew.

These were the Trials at which I, at age fifteen, made my breakthrough, coming in second in the 200 fly.

Instead of chasing our Olympic dreams together, Whitney and I, it was just me.

Those 2000 Trials were back in Indianapolis, at the same pool where Whitney, favored to make the team just four years before, had not. It took extraordinary courage for Whitney to show up there again. After I had placed second to Malchow and made the Sydney team, she made her way down to the pool deck and threw her arms around me. I knew I had made that 2000 team in no small part because of Whitney; she had shown me what kind of dedication and commitment it took.

Whitney's heartache was far from over, however. She spent the next couple of years wrestling with her conflicting feelings. On the one hand, she had done great things in swimming; she'd earned her way to the top of the national rankings, she had represented the United States on the world stage. On the other, girls she had raced were now representing the United States at major meets, and it was too tough to watch. Something she had loved had been taken from her and it wasn't her fault. She had been injured; this was no fault of will.

I would go to meets, in Sydney, for instance, at the 2000 Games, and my mom and Hilary were in the stands, but Whitney was not.

It wasn't that she was spiteful.

Far from it. She was hurting. And being at meets felt even more hurtful. It was simply too frustrating for her to sit in the stands and think how fast she could have gone if she'd only been able to train.

Time is a great healer. One day, she realized that she had done amazing things, had accomplished a lot, should be proud of herself. That's when she started going to more of my meets.

One of the first back was in Indianapolis, in 2003, the Duel in the Pool; the one Ian and many of the other Australian swimmers declined to attend. I won four events that day, including the family legacy, the 200 fly.

Now, when I look into the stands, I see Whitney and Hilary on either side of my mom. Knowing what it took to get Whitney there, how could I not be even more motivated?

•   •   •

Everyone makes mistakes. In November 2004, I made a big one. I drove after drinking. I should not have gotten behind the wheel. It was wrong. Wrong for so many reasons.

By way of explanation, not excuse: After the Athens Games ended, I was, for the first time in my life, on my own. No Mom, no Bob telling me what to do.

Almost as soon as I got back from Greece, I went on a tour with Ian Crocker and another American Olympic swim star, Lenny Krayzelburg. We traveled around the United States on a bus that slept twelve and that used to belong to David Copperfield, the magician. We would visit schools and conduct swim shows at local pools; the three of us would demonstrate stroke techniques, then race each other, different strokes from show to show. We would also take turns as anchors on relays made up of local kids.

From the time I was fourteen, I had been sensitive to back pain, mindful of what had sidelined Whitney. As the post-Athens exhibition made its way through Oregon, I felt something sharp on my right side. It did not feel good.

The pain went away on the next leg of the trip, a six-hundred-mile bus ride down to Sacramento. All the way, however, I was obsessing about me, about Whitney, about back pain. I was unsettled. I felt insecure.

The tour ended in early October, in Anaheim. Mom and Bob met me there. We flew to Indianapolis, to the FINA short-course world championships, held at Conseco Fieldhouse, an event one of my sponsors was helping to underwrite. I won the 200 free in an American record time. But then I felt it in my back, again.

I withdrew from the meet and went to Baltimore. An MRI showed what's called a *pars fracture,* from repeated bending and stretching. Maybe I'd had it since I was a kid; maybe not. The doctors told me to wear a removable brace for six weeks and stay out of the pool.

I didn't know what to do with myself. I had no structure, no rhythm, no routine to my days or my nights.

One of my good friends was in college at a town on Maryland's Eastern Shore and so we decided, that first weekend of November, to go out there. Road trip. I had just gotten my new car, a silver 2005 Range Rover. One of my friends made sure to tell me before we left: no drinking and driving. I said, come on, that's not me.

We hung out at a party. I had three beers. We decided to go get some food. I got behind the wheel of the Range Rover. A few blocks away, I rolled through a stop sign. The car coming down the street, as it turned out, was a Maryland state patrol car.

As soon as the lights on the police car started whirling, I knew I was in trouble. I immediately understood I had made a seriously stupid mistake. The trooper gave me a Breathalyzer test. My blood-alcohol reading measured 0.08, precisely the state standard for driving under the influence.

I was thoroughly ashamed.

My decision to drink and drive could have hurt someone. I was lucky it had not.

I was not yet twenty-one, the legal drinking age. I had flouted the law.

I had embarrassed myself, my family, my coach, and my team, just for starters.

I would have to be held accountable.

Who to call first?

Should I call my mom, who would yell at me and worry? Bob, who would yell at me but help me? Or Peter, who I knew would help?

I called Peter. He said, let me figure out what we ought to do next, I'll get back to you.

When I called Bob, who was at a meet in Wisconsin, he was supportive, but he also gave me the hard truth: "Michael, just because you want to blow off some steam doesn't mean you can be an idiot."

Then, face to face, I had to tell my mom.

She knew I had made a mistake. But that's not how she had raised me, to make that kind of mistake. I was so, so sorry. I was immature and I'd been stupid. That didn't change anything but that was the reality.

I felt I'd gone from seemingly being on top of the world—the Olympics in Athens had ended a little over two months before— to being in the deepest black hole on the face of the earth.

Peter, Bob, my mom, and I met to talk about what to do. I said, it's on me to tell people what I had done. I called friends and extended family. I also called reporters I had come to know to tell them what I had done, that I made a mistake, and that I wanted each of them to hear it from me. I sat there for hours.

The look on Bob's face never changed; he was extremely disappointed.

Mom started crying. That hurt worse, maybe, than anything. I had never seen my mother that upset. I vowed it would never happen again.

We worried that my sponsors might abandon me. None did.

A week after my arrest, USA Swimming held a fundraiser, an awards dinner called the Golden Goggles, in New York City. Everyone makes mistakes, but I just want you to know—I've never seen anything handled the way you've been handling it, I was told by Dick Ebersol, the NBC Sports chairman. It meant a great deal to me that he said so.

In late December, I went to court in Salisbury to plead guilty to driving while impaired. It was humbling indeed to walk into court, my every step recorded by television cameras. Inside, after my guilty plea, the state dropped its other charges; I was ordered to pay $305 in fines and court costs, to attend a meeting of Mothers Against Drunk Driving, and to speak at a number of schools about drinking, driving, and decision making.

The next April, back in Salisbury, I spoke to the seniors at Parkside High School. It was a few days before their prom. Have fun, I said, but be responsible. You need to set goals and keep in mind that the decisions you make can determine whether you will achieve those goals, I said.

The night that I got behind the wheel after drinking, I said, I had lost sight of my goals. I was not thinking, as I should have been, about Beijing and 2008. "In order to make good decisions, you really have to see the whole picture," I said. "I guess you could say my head wasn't really on straight . . . my goals were not in order when I got behind the wheel."

I'd like to think that maybe I helped at least one person make a decision not to drive after drinking. Maybe at Parkside High School, maybe somewhere else. If even one person has looked at me, or heard about what I did, and shuddered, and thought, no, I don't want to go through that, then it was all worth it.

In no way would I wish the experience, any and all of it, on anyone, but it changed my life. It reminded me in the most direct way possible that no one is so important that he deserves to be, or will be, treated any differently than anybody else.

The experience also led me, in one of those connections in life that, after it happens, seems like one of those things that was all along somehow meant to be, to Greg Harden, who is an associate athletic director at Michigan and the school's director of athletic counseling. I went to check in with him after I'd moved to

Ann Arbor. He knew what had occurred. Look, he said, one of the biggest things I'll tell you is this: Whenever you make a mistake, learn from it. As long as you can learn from every mistake, he said, you'll be fine. You can make a million mistakes, just not the same one twice.

Greg Harden gave me good advice. I am grateful.

• • •

Such good advice and yet, at least when it came to swimming, apparently just to swimming, I already knew not to be reckless.

I had learned that lesson the hard way, too, after my first Olympics, in the way I approached the 200 fly in particular.

Yes, I set the world record in Austin. Yes, I lowered it in Fukuoka.

But for a year after that?

At those 2002 Fort Lauderdale nationals, I had such a great meet except for the 200 fly, at least by the standards that mattered, mine and Bob's. I set out to break the record. I did not get there, and after the race I put my head in my hands. At that moment, I was only beginning to understand what not training diligently in the butterfly would yield. Bob directed my training sets, of course, but when it came to the fly he would every now and then give me a choice of doing extra butterfly sets at the close of practice. I usually said, no, thanks. It was, after all, my best stroke. At the end of a workout, I was genuinely tired.

Bob had let me learn the hard way that there was no substitute for the hard work it would always take to get better.

Later that summer, at the Pan Pacs in Yokohama, Malchow beat me in the 200 fly. If I needed an even more blunt reminder, now I had it.

I hated losing.

I also hated hearing Bob say, "I told you so."

After that, Bob gave me punishing butterfly sets. Through Athens, I devoured them. That is what Bob wanted—my best effort. There's a huge difference in not swimming well because of a technical glitch and not swimming well for lack of effort. Bob knows what's what. What he wants and expects are as many consecutive days of first-rate training as possible.

Bob also, quite deliberately, would arrange practices, schedules, workouts, drills, whatever he could think of, around the idea of being uncomfortable.

His thinking always has been to put his swimmers through every scenario possible. You're tired; you feel you can't move; you're truly hurting. That's when he would throw down especially hard sets. Bob wanted to gauge not only how I felt under pressure but, more important, how I responded under pressure. If I could deal with whatever it was when I was tired, I could deal with anything that came my way. Because that is the real definition of a champion, someone who can deal with any obstacle that comes his or her way, can deal with any situation at any given point.

Michael Jordan was so sick with the stomach flu before game five of the 1997 NBA Finals that he hardly slept the night before. He was exhausted and dehydrated. He played 44 minutes and scored 38 points, and his Chicago Bulls won the game by two points.

A champion can deal with any kind of pressure.

It wasn't just the intensity of the practices, however, that made up the Bowman approach to stress management. It was anything and everything. It was why, going all the way back to 1999 and the nationals in Minneapolis, we dragged back to the hotel to get me a swimsuit.

In Baltimore, I never had a lane to swim in by myself. I swam four or five to a lane, like everyone else. No special treatment, not after the 2000 Olympics, nothing.

That trip to the Bahamas, the same day I did a lengthy photo shoot with the dolphin? That day started off with a morning practice. The photo shoot followed. In the afternoon, instead of enjoying the island scenery or lounging poolside with a fruity drink, Bob ordered up practice. He knows that I shiver if I stay in cold water too long, and it was a cold, gray day in a pool warmed only by solar heat. Would I tough it out? Yes.

In Australia in 2003, Bob deliberately asked our driver to show up late. That way I had to spend more time waiting at the pool, and we missed dinner. I ordered pizza. That same trip, he stepped on my goggles, on purpose. I had to make do.

A power outage one day at the pool in Michigan meant nothing. We swam in the dark. That was good, Bob said. Made you swim by feel. Forced you to count your strokes.

Back in Australia in 2007, at the Worlds in Melbourne, my goggles started sliding down my face as I turned into the final 50, the freestyle leg, of the 200 IM. The goggles filled with water. I couldn't see Lochte or Cseh at all. I knew that I had turned about a half-second ahead and so I just drove for home. When I touched and turned, I blinked and blinked and blinked until I could see the board: 1:54.98, a new world record.

So what if I couldn't see? What's important now? Getting it done, no matter what.

•　•　•

The night before that 200 IM in Melbourne, I swam the finals of the 200 fly. This is how good that race was. Afterward, Bob just smiled at me.

I was timed in that 200 fly in Melbourne in 1:52.09, not just a world record but by 1.62 seconds. The runner-up in the race, Wu Peng of China, touched more than three seconds behind. Typically, when a record is broken, the line that gets superimposed on the television broadcast or on the arena big board runs just behind a swimmer's fingers; records are usually taken down by hundredths of tenths of a second. In this instance, the line was near my feet.

I felt like I was twelve again, in the sense that you break records by that much only when you're twelve.

It was the sort of thing that made newspapers and television around the world take notice of swimming, in a non-Olympic year, no less. On ESPN, they debated my place in sports history. The back page of the *Herald Sun,* Australia's largest newspaper, featured a photo of me rising out of the water in midstroke; the headline reached across the entire page of the tabloid, just one word: "Greatest." My hometown newspaper, the *Baltimore Sun,* called it "stunning" and offered comparisons to Bob Beamon's history-making long jump, 29 feet, 2½ inches, two feet past what had been the world record, at the 1968 Mexico City Olympics. Mark Schubert, our U.S. team coach, told the Baltimore paper that what I did might have been even better. "I don't think it's comparable to Beamon's performance because that was a lifetime, out-of-body experience that we never saw again," he said, meaning Beamon never again jumped that far. "I think we're going to see an even better time from Michael. I just think he's that good."

Honestly, in the warm-ups before the 200 fly final in Melbourne I had felt crummy. My arms felt sore. I had gone 1:43.86 in the 200 free just the day before.

Once I got up on the blocks, I had to get over all that. How I felt then was not the least bit important to what was possible now. It was time to go out and race, the weight training obviously making a huge, huge difference in what I was now able to do.

The time in Melbourne surprised me, but not the record itself. I had realized the month before, at the annual midwinter meet in Missouri, that I was on the verge of something special. I showed up at the Missouri meet with a full goatee. My hair was hanging out of my cap. I was obviously not shaved and certainly not tapered. Even so, I had gone out that night and lowered my world record in the 200 fly. In Victoria, at the Pan Pacs in 2006, I had gone 1:53.80; in Missouri, I took nine-tenths of a second off that, dropping the record to 1:53.71.

To go under that in Melbourne by more than a second and a

half is why I had enormous expectations for myself in this race in Beijing, why I put 1:51.1 on my 2008 goal sheet.

At the Olympic final, immediately before the starter called, "Take your marks," I pushed my goggles to my eyes. Not sure, even now, why.

I race in metallic Speedo goggles, a model called the "Speed Socket." I also race in two caps. The sequence goes like this: I put the goggles on, then one cap, then the other. That way the goggles are secure.

Nothing seemed amiss.

Obviously, however, something was wrong. Fernando and Mona could see that all the way from Norway.

At the beep, immediately after I dove in, the goggles started leaking. I couldn't tell whether the seal had broken on the top or bottom.

That wasn't important. What was important was to go.

When I turned at 50, the thought flashed through my mind that maybe the leak wouldn't be that bad. It seemed manageable.

At 100, though, things started getting more and more blurry. Just after that, as I made my way up the pool to the far wall, with perhaps 75 meters to go in the race, the cups of the goggles filled entirely. I could not see.

I could not see the line on the bottom of the pool. I could not see the black T that marks the coming of the wall. I could not see anybody else in any other lane. I could not see.

This wasn't football, or basketball. I didn't have the luxury of calling a time-out.

I couldn't take the goggles off and swim old school because the goggles were trapped under both caps.

This was an Olympic final. I had to go. At that instant, that's what was the most important thing. I had to go hard and fast.

There was no time to think about anything. But what was there to think about? I was the farthest thing from freaked out. This very thing had happened to me just the year before, in Melbourne, in the 200 IM finals. It happens sometimes in swimming. It was happening to me now.

In the 200 fly, there's a regular and predictable progression of strokes as the race goes along. That is, there are so many strokes per length of the pool, the number typically going up by one per lap because of the inevitable demands on the body and the fatigue.

The first length usually takes sixteen strokes. The second, eighteen; the gap is two because the race starts with a dive. The third length usually goes nineteen strokes. The final length, nineteen or twenty.

When my goggles filled, I was on the third length. Thus, the magic number to get to the far wall was nineteen, maybe twenty. Because my goggles were already leaking before the turn, anticipating the crisis, I had started a stroke count as soon as I made the turn into that third length.

Four or five strokes into that third length—that's where it all closed in and I could no longer see.

Sixteen. Seventeen. Eighteen. Nineteen. Where was that wall?

Twenty, and a glide; there, there it was.

Perfect. I had spaced it perfectly, the glide carrying me into the wall and a touch. I hadn't come into the wall in midstroke or hammered into it or jammed my fingers or bent back my wrist or any of the other things that could have gone wrong. In Omaha, Emily Silver had broken her right hand after swimming into the wall at the finish of the 50-meter free semis. It put her out of the pool for more than a week.

In the stands, Whitney was concerned. His stroke is tight, she said to Mom.

Bob was also wondering what was going on. The way we had planned it, I should have been much farther ahead, pushing for 1:51. Bob's mind had already started racing. Maybe, he figured, for some inexplicable reason I was looking ahead to the 800 relay, which both of us knew I was going to have to race later that morning, about fifty-six minutes after the end of the 200 fly, and was just going hard enough in the fly to get the job done.

Little did he know that I wasn't looking anywhere. I couldn't see. It was as bad as it could get.

Coming down the homestretch, I was just hoping I'd given myself enough of a lead so that nobody could run me down.

Seventeen. Eighteen.

I could hear the crowd roaring. For me? For someone else? Was it close?

Nineteen. Twenty. Wall, wall, wall, where was that last wall?

One more stroke. Give it one more stroke, twenty-one and reach for it, glide just a touch.

There, there it was! I felt it with my hands. Again, I had timed it just right. I didn't ram into the wall with my shoulder or, worse, my head. I reached for it, hands out in front, and got it with my fingers.

Just the way I would have tried to do it if I could have seen what I was doing.

With my right hand, I reached up and ripped off my goggles. Both the caps came flying off, too, into the water with the goggles. I leaned on the lane line with my right arm, blinking hard. I tossed the caps behind me onto the deck with my left hand, picked up the goggles with my right and flung them behind me, too, then looked up, breathing hard, shaking my head from side to side, squinting at the scoreboard.

Next to my name it said, 1. It also said WR, a world record, 1:52.03. Incredible.

I was simultaneously thrilled and, candidly, frustrated as I got out of the pool and said to Bob, "I couldn't see anything."

I was not put out so much at the wardrobe malfunction—stuff happens—but frustrated at the opportunity lost. My fly had come on so strong in 2007 and 2008. I had extraordinary confidence I could go super-fast at the Olympics. I had, and yet I could have gone faster. There was no doubt in my mind that I could have gone faster. No doubt at all.

And it was natural, there in the pool, to wonder, would I have an opportunity ever again to swim this race so fast?

I shook it off.

What was important now was taking the briefest of moments to appreciate what I had just done.

Nine swims down, eight to go.

Four for four in gold-medal swims. Cseh had gone four seconds faster than he had ever gone before, and still come in second, in 1:52.70; Takeshi Matsuda of Japan went two seconds better than his prior best, and came in third, in 1:52.97. The field I had just beaten was so fast that bronze in Athens would not even have gotten a spot in the final eight in Beijing.

And now, of course I had ten gold medals over my three Olympics, more than anyone else in history. I thought, wow, the "greatest Olympian of all time," that's a pretty cool title.

It was too dizzying, way too much for me to appreciate right then and there. I had to go swim a relay. That relay was truly what was important now.

In the stands, meanwhile, Hilary said to Mom, it's ironic, isn't it? The 200 fly got Michael to the Olympics for the first time. The 200 fly is the event in which he got his first world record. It was the event that made him somebody in the international swim scene. Now that's the event that launched Michael into history with his tenth Olympic medal.

Mom thought about that for a moment amid the din there in the Water Cube. She looked at Hilary and said, where do you come up with these things?

5

CONFIDENCE: THE 800 FREE RELAY

My BlackBerry buzzed before I set out for the Water Cube the morning of the 200 fly and the 800 freestyle relay, a text message from back home: "Dude, it's ridiculous how many times I have to see your ugly face." Then came another message: "It's time to be the best ever."

I had to laugh.

I laughed a lot at the Beijing Games. It felt different than in Athens and that's because it was different. The 2008 Games were my third Olympics; I knew what to expect. I had been through the media storm in 2004, for instance, so I knew what was coming in 2008. That time, I was a deer in headlights; I had never gotten that much media attention. Also, in Athens, I was only nineteen. Maybe I was too young to appreciate fully what the Olympics were all about. It's like all the little lessons Bob and I had been working on for fully a dozen years; they were all there to see in Beijing, on display in particular in that 800 relay.

I knew, for example, how to conserve energy through a whole meet, whether it was seven, eight, or nine days. Related to that was the furious work I had put in during the hours in the pool and the weight room. If few people truly understood how hard I had worked, the grueling nature of the workouts Bob had put me and the others in our training group in Michigan through, the endurance that I had built would reveal itself in the relays.

Part of it, as well, was how I had grown up since Athens. I was now twenty-three. I had moved to Michigan, lived on my own, made mistakes, endured health scares. My relationship with Bob was forced to evolve, and it did. That maturity would be on ample display in the relays as well; we had to swim with passion but at the same time swim smart.

Then, too, there were the relationships with my teammates, which mattered to me immensely, and the opportunity to take all three relay titles back to the United States. That also mattered to me intensely. The 800 was not likely to be a replay of the 400 earlier in the week. What could be, after Jason had seemingly captivated the entire world with his anchor leg? But that didn't mean it could or should be taken for granted. And in this 800 we had a very definite goal, to do something no team of four guys swimming four laps apiece had ever done: break seven minutes.

We wanted to go six-something.

This relay had an incredible Olympic history. We wanted to make a little history of our own.

$$\bullet \quad \bullet \quad \bullet$$

Before I found a place of my own in Michigan, I had to bunk with Bob. It was the most miserable month ever, for him and for me.

This arrangement occupied late November and early December 2004. Bob wanted to watch over me. I didn't want to be watched. The DUI had given him more reason to watch me more closely. I felt bad enough about it already.

"Are you eating enough?" Bob would ask. "Sleeping enough?"

Stop treating me like an eleven-year-old, I finally said after one too many of these sorts of questions.

The television was his television; we watched what he wanted to watch. I would retreat to my room to play video games or to hack around on my computer.

Finally, we got into it big time. I couldn't stand even one more second.

"I'm out of here!" I said.

"Okay," Bob said. "Don't let the door hit you on your way out."

"Good," I said right back, ever so cleverly. "I'm going back to Baltimore."

I threw my things in the car and walked out, then called my mom.

"Now, Michael," she said, calmly, "what are the advantages of coming home? Of course you can come back, but would you train here? Are you going to find a new coach? What about school?"

I turned around. I even showed up at practice. But the feeling that he was making every decision in my life for me had hardly gone away. I had to get some space.

A few days later, I signed the papers to buy a condo near campus. I wanted out from Bob so badly that I slept there on an air mattress helpfully supplied by a Michigan assistant coach.

The dynamic was complicated further, and to be truthful, aggravated, by my back problems. At the very same time that I wanted the adult freedom of being on my own, I also needed Bob's reassurance. Little wonder things were edgy. Another MRI in early December offered clearer evidence of a stress fracture. I was given three options: stop training for six months; practice through the pain with uncertain short- and long-term consequences to my discs; surgery, with at least three months of no swimming. What was unsaid, of course, was that my entire career might be at risk—even if it was being thought by me and by anyone who knew Whitney and the family history.

More opinions were sought.

In the meantime, as I rested, my symptoms—just like that—went away. We began to incorporate cross-training and core work into my training, meaning push-ups, pull-ups, sit-ups, sessions with a medicine ball.

And I was left to figure out how to live this new life in Ann Arbor.

At first, I had no dishes. Having gone to the grocery store for milk and cereal, I did have something to eat. What to eat it in? A Gatorade container would have to do. I poured the cereal in there, sloshed the milk in on top, swirled it all around and drank it all down.

Soon enough, I had dishes. I put them in the dishwasher, then poured liquid hand soap in the soap tray. That led to a bubble bath all over the kitchen floor.

As time went along, I did become more accomplished in the house, sort of. At one point, the smoke detector started singing. I hadn't been cooking. I didn't smell anything burning. What could it be?

I called Bob. "Michael," he said, "when was the last time you changed the batteries in the smoke detector?"

"You need to do that?"

I took a handful of courses—at some point, I would like to get my college degree—and got the Michigan "M" tattooed on my left hip, a counterpoint to the Olympic rings on my right.

After getting a crash course after Athens in fame, I was mostly allowed to be alone in Ann Arbor. Nobody bothered the football players much; in the same way, I was mostly left to be myself and be by myself, if that's what I wanted. At the same time, I had to learn to juggle sponsor commitments around the country even as Peter and I weighed a seemingly relentless flood of invites from anyone and everyone interested in a piece of me, everything from the Miss USA pageant (yes) to bar mitzvahs (not really).

That winter, Bob and I wanted to be both cautious with my training, yet as aggressive as we could be. In March 2005, it was back to Indianapolis for the meet that would qualify swimmers for that year's Worlds in Montreal. I won the 200 IM, out-touched Ian Crocker in the 100 fly, and then, in the 100 free, set a personal-best, 49-flat, holding off Jason Lezak, who, like me, had not been training his hardest over that winter. At that Indy meet, my back felt fine; the times and the wins were not nearly as reassuring as that simple fact.

By the time we got to Montreal, I had for the year put in maybe half the miles in the pool I had done in years prior. I did win gold medals there. But it was clear after the 400 free prelim disaster, then that same week losing emphatically to Ian Crocker in the 100 fly, that I was not where I wanted to be. Montreal was a wake-up call.

"Phelps flop," screamed one newspaper headline. A columnist for the *Montreal Gazette* wrote, "Visitors to the World Aquatics Championships the past week have been wondering why the city of Montreal has lifeguards posted around the pools. Any chance you saw Michael Phelps struggle home over the final two lengths of his 400-metre freestyle heat yesterday? The U.S. superstar was breathtaking in the worst way imaginable, failing to make the eight-man final while looking like a weary age-grouper . . ."

The only thing I could do was use it as motivation.

• • •

Though I was taking some courses, loved going to Michigan football games, said "Go Blue!" when I was honored with an ESPY for what I'd done in Athens, it took me a while to learn how to fit in at Michigan. I was never going to be just a regular college kid, not just another member of the high-performance training group—called Club Wolverine—at the pool.

Because I had turned professional years before, I was not representing Michigan at dual meets with the likes of Wisconsin or swimming for the Wolverines at the Big Ten or NCAA championships.

In its way, this was another challenge. If I didn't have the academic record of the college guys who were, for example, engineering majors, was it weirder for them to be in the same pool with me?

Then came the sudden death of Eric Namesnik in January 2006, which jolted everyone who'd ever had a connection to Michigan swimming and, for that matter, anyone with any connection of any kind to swimming, or even to the Olympics. Twice the Olympic silver medalist in the 400 IM, Snik, which is what everyone called him, died four days after being critically injured in an early-morning car crash on an icy road. I had first met Snik when I was eleven; he was only thirty-five, with a wife and two children, when he passed away. His favorite saying: "Dream no small dreams, for they have no power to move the hearts of men."

That April, meanwhile, Erik Vendt showed up in Ann Arbor, intent on resuming his racing career. I could not have been more thrilled. I needed, to use Bob's analogy, to make a considerable deposit into the fitness bank. And no one had ever trained harder than Erik Vendt.

Erik had taken time off after Athens. He'd gone backpacking around Europe, then moved to New York. There he worked at a swim school, teaching kids. The kids' attitude completely changed his. Before, he had looked at swimming as racing, placing, and medals. Working with the kids, he saw the success and pride of getting in the pool for the first time, getting their face in the water for that first time. Seeing their excitement and joy made him excited all over again about swimming. He was toying with the idea of coming back when, listening to the Olympic theme song from the telecast of the Winter Games from Torino, Italy, in February 2006, he literally got chills up and down his spine and thought to himself, I guess I'm not done yet. So he called Jon, and said, do you think I could get in with the Club Wolverine crew? Get back in here, Jon said.

Erik, who's from Massachusetts, had gone to college at USC, swimming under Mark Schubert. Mark had left USC to become the U.S. team national coach; with Bob and Jon, Erik figured he'd get punished in practice just like he would have with Mark but, at Michigan, he'd also get more of an emphasis on weight training, which I was aggressively starting to work on that year, too.

If I was willing to work hard in practice, Erik had perhaps an even greater appetite for it. He set out to remake himself into a freestyler instead of an all-arounder in the individual medleys, everything from the 200 free to 1500, no small thing because he was himself a two-time Olympic silver medalist in the 400 IM. And Erik just ate up whatever Bob threw at him. If, on a scale of one to ten, I was now turning in consistent eights at practice, very few sinking to a two, rising every now and then to a ten, Eric was maybe a nine each and every day. I had, and still have, never seen anyone work out so hard and be so competitive, both in workouts and in the racing itself.

Aside from that, Erik and I had history together, going back to the 2000 Olympic team and our one-two finish in the 400 IM in Athens. He was four years older, which suited me perfectly, because at North Baltimore I was always the young kid hanging out with the older guys. He would motivate me when I needed motivation. He never held anything back, always told me exactly how it was. I sometimes didn't like to hear whatever it was Erik had for me, but better to hear it from him than one more time from Bob. Erik would also mediate when Bob and I had one of our periodic moments. On the road, Erik and I took to rooming together.

Without Erik Vendt, there was no way I could have gotten through the years from Athens to Beijing.

All of us in Club Wolverine pushed each other hard. In Baltimore, I had been used to winning every practice set, it seemed. Not here. Davis Tarwater had emerged as one of the best in the country in the butterfly. He and I would go at it in fly sets; I had never had anyone go with me in those sets but, literally, he and I would be swimming side by side in what seemed like every set. Peter Vanderkaay was a 2004 Olympic teammate of mine from Athens. Klete Keller, who trained in Ann Arbor until moving to Southern California, had been a teammate in both Sydney and Athens.

This was no boys-only club. Katie Carroll was a Big East swim champion at Notre Dame. Kaitlin Sandeno won four Olympic medals, one in Sydney, three in Athens. As we got closer to the Trials in Omaha, we were joined by Michigan high school star Allison Schmitt. At first, there were some raised eyebrows in what was largely a group of post-grads, of older swimmers, about Allison's arrival. She was going to go on to college in the fall: Did she really belong? She quickly not only proved that she did belong, she brought immense life to the party. In truth, she brought all of us closer.

Jon may have sometimes affectionately referred to Kaitlin as "the Princess," but the girls got no breaks. No one wanted any. We were all there to train for the Trials and the Games, as the clock across the pool counted down the time, in days, hours, minutes, seconds, down to tenths of a second, before the start of the Beijing Olympics.

• • •

Morning practice at the Canham pool got started at either seven or seven-thirty, depending on the season, and went for roughly two hours.

If it was seven, my alarm would go off at six-twenty, maybe six-thirty. I still was not a morning person. I wouldn't be out of bed until six-forty-five. That gave me just enough time to grab something I could eat on the run, get to the pool, throw my suit on, walk onto the deck, get my equipment, and be ready to dive in. I would practice most mornings in a swimming brief, what the rest of the world might call a Speedo; they were Speedos, of course, often a model called the Flip Turn, and I particularly liked one with yellow moons and yellow unicorn heads set against a magenta background. It was so hideously ugly that it actually had tons of style. Same for a neon-green one plastered with red cherries.

There were afternoon practices as well, along with weights three times a week; and "dryland," push-ups, pull-ups, medicine ball or yoga, and, depending on the time of year, separate cardio work.

Bob spelled out in meticulous detail how each practice would go. He wrote the program out in longhand, then made copies for each of us and for the coaches. It was way too complicated to memorize. The trick was to dip your own copy in the pool water, which would give it just enough stick to get stuck to the metal guardrail at the end of each of our lanes. Each workout also included a notation in the corner: how many days to go until the Trials in Omaha as well as the Games in Beijing.

There were kicking drills. Work with kickboards, snorkels and paddles. With fins. Parachutes.

There were no bathroom breaks. At least for the guys. If you had to go, you went, right there in the pool.

Around all this working out there had to be resting, noon-time naps, especially.

And there had to be eating. Lots of eating. Thousands of calories. During the Olympics, that rumor got started that I was inhaling twelve thousand calories a day. It seemed to spread like wildfire. It's just not true.

Maybe eight to ten thousand calories per day. But not twelve thousand.

When I was in Baltimore, later in my high-school years, I used to go after practice every morning to a restaurant named Pete's.

Breakfast there went like this: three sandwiches made of fried eggs, cheese, lettuce, tomato, fried onion, and mayonnaise. An omelet. A bowl of grits. Three slices of French toast with powdered sugar. And, as a kicker, three chocolate chip pancakes.

In Ann Arbor, my days started before that morning practice with a PowerBar, a bagel, a bowl of cereal, or a Pop-Tart. Just something quick and easy, some carbs before working out.

After the morning swim, I would go out for a real breakfast to places I soon discovered as I found my way around Ann Arbor.

If it was Benny's Family Dining, I liked to slide into a booth near the front, away from the cigarette smokers. Breakfast would start with a bowl of rice pudding. Then: three eggs over easy, hash browns, sausages, and wheat toast. Maybe a side of bacon. Sometimes, I'd go for the Mexican or Southern omelet. If I was off to Mr. Greek's, I would have a Greek's skillet: scrambled eggs, gyro meat, feta cheese, tomato, and onion, with bacon or sausage on the side. Plus a short stack of banana chocolate-chip pancakes. If I was really hungry, I might also get an order of cheese fries. At ten in the morning, cheese fries at the same meal with pancakes. Sounds so bad. Tasted so good.

The Maize and Blue Deli Delicatessen was another regular stop, for stuffed sandwiches, two or three. Maybe the No. 29, Jennifer's Dream: turkey, provolone, mayo, Dijon mustard, lettuce, tomato, and pickle on grilled white bread. Or the No. 30, Forever Turkey: turkey, provolone cheese, Dijon mustard, tomato, and onion on grilled sourdough rye. Or possibly the Maize 'N Blue Special, No. 69: roast beef, smoked turkey, cheddar, Jarlsberg cheese, mustard, lettuce, tomato, onion, and mild pepper on a sub roll.

If I didn't want to sit down, I'd hop by Bruegger's, the bagel place, for two or three sausage, egg, and cream cheese bagels to go. Sausage, egg, and cream cheese. Tastes great.

Whether I ate at one of my favorite places or grabbed the

bagels to go, the next destination was always home, to rest before the afternoon workout, usually four to six P.M. After I'd get up for that, I'd have something small to eat, maybe a sandwich, or left-over pizza, or a bowl of cereal.

At night, it was off to the Produce Station, one of those grocery stores that sells every different kind of fruit and vegetable as well as ready-made dinners like chicken or steak. If not there, to a Mexican restaurant called the Prickly Pear for the buffalo enchiladas. A place called Casey's had awesome burgers.

I had my few spots in Ann Arbor, and at those spots I had my selections on each of the menus. It got pretty quickly to the point where I didn't even bother looking at a menu. I got the same thing every time. It's always been like that with me: At that meet in Federal Way when I was not yet fifteen, I ate every single meal, twenty-one over seven days, at a place called Mitzell's, next to our hotel, and at every single meal I had clam chowder as an appetizer and cheesecake for dessert.

Erik, meanwhile, after moving to Ann Arbor, tried to go organic. When I wake up, he used to say, I feel it, I feel alive.

I felt alive, too, even if I wasn't going organic. I ate whatever I wanted, really. But I also ate my salads, my greens, making sure to give my body everything it needed.

But not twelve thousand calories per day. If I had done that, I would seriously have fit the funny headline in the *New York Post* during the Beijing Olympics that reported I was eating that much: "Boy Gorge."

* * *

As intense as the pace in Ann Arbor could be, swimming maybe 55 miles per week, it was a piece of cheesecake indeed when compared to our training sessions at the USOC base in Colorado Springs, altitude 6,100 feet. Those camps were, in a word, brutal.

We went there three times in the eighteen months preceding the

2008 Trials, once after the Melbourne Worlds, once as the calendar was turning from 2007 to 2008, then one last time, as April 2008 stretched into May.

The point of these excursions to Colorado was twofold: Swimming at altitude helps build endurance. And being at the USOC base makes you focus completely on swimming, because there is nothing else there to do. It's a place with absolutely no distractions. You swim, you eat, you sleep. Literally, that's all there is to do. Bob likes it that way. He has a captive audience.

The idea that you could ratchet up your endurance by training at altitude became widespread in track and field after Kip Keino, who had been born and raised at elevation in western Kenya, ran to Olympic glory in Mexico City at the 1968 Summer Games. From then on it was only a matter of time until it spread as well to other sports, including swimming.

It's easy to explain why altitude training works. Red blood cells carry oxygen; the cells in the muscles demand that oxygen. The more red blood cells you have, the more oxygen you can carry to the muscles. Training at altitude builds more red blood cells. Thus, back at sea level for competitions, the harder, faster, stronger—whatever—you should be able to go.

The trick at altitude is to ride the fine line between doing enough but not too much. Thus the coaching dilemma: How much to challenge each of us without anyone breaking down? The working theory for Bob and Jon was that we would do just as much work as if we were still in Michigan, but instead of two swims per day it would be spread over three—the shorter sessions being less of a challenge to the immune system. Even so, Bob would spend most of his time in Colorado worried about us going over the edge because once you're over, it's over. You don't come back, at least not quickly.

Bob's mentor, Paul Bergen, believed in the benefits of training at altitude; that led Bob to the altitude-training protocols developed by Gennady Touretsky, the former Soviet national sprint coach who, from a base in Australia, directed Alexander Popov, the Russian swimmer who won the sprints, both the 50 and 100, at both the 1992 Barcelona and 1996 Atlanta Olympics. Bob managed to get copies of what Touretsky had done. Using that as a starting point, then mixing in Jon's proven success in designing programs to hone middle-distance swimmers, Bob designed his own plan that pushed each one of us to our limits.

Each Colorado trip runs for three weeks and includes roughly seventy swimming, conditioning, or weightlifting workouts. Everything gets carefully plotted out on a Cambridge planning pad, on graph paper, that Bob buys at CVS drugstores, eight at a time; he always buys them in bulk because he's afraid one day they're going to stop selling them.

At the final camp, the one in April and May, we swam, all in, about 200,000 meters, or just under 125 miles. If we were running on the roads, that would have been the equivalent of nearly five marathons.

The push is both in the mileage itself and in the intensity of the workouts. There were days of aerobic work, which for us meant a workout where we were not breathing hard and our pulse would average 120 to 140 beats per minute, alternating with days of anaerobic work, swims where we were breathing harder and our heart rates were pushed up to 175 to 200 beats. The area in between aerobic and anaerobic work, 150 to 175 beats, is called the "anaerobic threshold"; that threshold zone, according to Jon, provides the most optimal intensity for improving endurance. It was obviously critical to find that zone. Complicating things just a bit, that zone was different for each of us. How to find it? It was done in Ann Arbor the week before leaving for Colorado. Each of us was put through a timed swim, 300 meters ten times; the results were fed into a computer program of Jon's design; the program calculated the 100-meter threshold pace.

Altitude added a two-second difference. At sea level, my threshold before the last trip to Colorado was 1:05.7; at altitude, it then became 1:07.7. Peter and Erik were training for longer distances than I was. Erik's threshold at sea level, for instance, was 1:03.5; at altitude, it became 1:05.5.

When we got into the pool in Colorado, we would then each be assigned the same general workout but be expected to finish laps at times that were calculated from each individual threshold. So, for example, if it was Monday afternoon of the first week, the main swim would be called a rainbow set, when we progressed through a color code from the computer printout doing 4,000 meters, forty 100s. The 4,000 would be broken down into five groups of eight swims; after each 100 we earned a slight rest period, 12 to 19 seconds, depending on where it was in the sequence.

Each of us would be told to do two of those five groups below the threshold, what Bob and Jon called the white, then pink pace; then one at threshold pace, red; then two sets above threshold pace, blue and purple, the colors getting darker in the way your skin might show signs of hard work and lack of oxygen.

The white pace for me, then, would be eight laps holding a time of 1:08.3 per 100; pink, 1:06; red, 1:04.8; blue, 1:02.7; purple, 1:00.5. Erik and Peter would have their own times.

The red pace, 1:04.8, doesn't correlate exactly with the 1:07.7 threshold time because I wouldn't be asked to swim the set continuously; instead, I was doing it in intervals, the computer figuring out the difference.

It's physically demanding and perhaps even more so mentally.

Coming into Omaha, however, we knew we were in great shape. It showed in the 200 free finals. I won, and Peter came in second. Erik came in sixth, a finish that got him onto the 2008 U.S. team and meant he would be swimming, at the least, in the prelims of the 800 relay in Beijing. He was pumped. For everything he had done in his career, Erik had never been on an Olympic relay. Not even once, and when we were sitting around the hotel room in Omaha before the 200 free final, he asked me, what do you think it's going to take to make it?

1:46, I said.

I can do that, he said.

Hop a wave that first 100, then destroy it coming home, I said.

Erik finished in 1:46.95. At 150, he said after the race, he not only could hear the crowd roaring, he could feel the roar in the pool. The last 15 meters, he didn't risk even one breath; he just put his head down and went for it. He said afterward, "If I pass out, I pass out." Better to have finished sixth and passed out afterwards than get seventh, he figured.

He did not pass out.

Klete came in fourth; he was in, too, along with two more up-and-coming talents from the University of Texas, Ricky Berens and Dave Walters, Ricky finishing third, Dave fifth.

As it turned out, Erik did not make the team in the 1500, to his, and pretty much everyone else's, surprise. Erik had come down from altitude and gone 14:46.78 at the Santa Clara meet in May, a U.S. Open record in the 1500; he finished an easy first, by 12 seconds, in the 1500 qualifying heat in Omaha. It seemed a foregone conclusion that he would not only win, he might set a record, especially when he told me the day before the finals, I'm feeling so good, so fresh.

That 1500 final was scheduled for the last day of the Trials, after I had finished my swims. Walking around the arena before the race, thinking Erik might finish in the low 14:40s, I ran into his parents, who said, well, how do you think he's going to do?

Really well, I said.

It just didn't turn out that way. Two-thirds of the way through the race, as Erik kept dropping farther and farther back, I found Bob and Jon poolside and I said, why is this happening?

No idea, each of them said. His warm-up was fine, his splits awesome.

After the race, Erik answered questions from the press for a long time. I waited for him. When he finished and got to me, I said, "You all right?"

"I don't know what it was," he said. "I felt so good today. But as soon as I dove in, I just didn't have it."

We stood there and hugged each other. Then he walked off. There wasn't anything more to say.

At least he was on the team. And in the relay pool. I was fired up about that. I was either going to be swimming with him, or for him.

• • •

Before the 400 free relay in Beijing, there is absolutely no question that the most exciting relay I had ever taken part in was the 800 free relay in Athens. There was also no question that this particular event had a special place in the tradition and culture of American swimming.

Before that Athens relay, for instance, Eddie showed us video of the 800 relay final from the 1984 Los Angeles Games. What a race. This was one of the few events at those Olympics unaffected by the Soviet-led boycott; everyone knew all along it was going to come down to the Americans and the West Germans, with Michael Gross. Coming into the Games, the Germans held the world record; in the prelims, a U.S. team broke it.

And then, for the finals, what strategy. The day before, Gross had won the 200 free in world-record time; American Michael Heath had come in second. An hour before the relay, Gross had to swim the 100 fly finals, which he won in another world record, out-touching Pablo Morales of the United States. Normally, the American coaches would have Heath, who had obviously just proven he was the fastest guy on the U.S. team at 200 meters, swim the anchor, matching him up against Gross. Given that Gross was so super-fast, though, the U.S. coaches switched it up. They put Heath first, with the idea that he would build up the biggest lead he could. The other two would try to push the lead. Then it was hold on and see what Gross had in him.

Bruce Hayes was told he'd be swimming the anchor leg; the year before, Hayes had anchored the winning 800 relay at the Pan American Games. Jeff Float, fourth in the 200 free behind Gross, swam the third leg; David Larson pulled the second.

Float had lost most of the hearing in both ears after coming down with viral meningitis at the age of thirteen months. The crowd was so loud during his swim that even he—in the water, no less—could hear the roar.

The American strategy had been to give Hayes a lead of about three seconds at takeoff. It was only about a second and a half. Gross made all of that up in the first 50. At 100 he passed Hayes. At 150, Gross had a lead of maybe two feet. But then, Hayes turned it on. At the Trials, Hayes had finished third in the 200 free; the 800 relay was thus the only event he had qualified for; he had spent training time since practicing his finishing touch. Practice paid off. Gross swam what was then the fastest 200 relay leg ever. But at the final wall, Hayes outtouched Gross by four-hundredths of a second. The Americans were Grossbusters, the new world-record holders by more than three seconds, in 7:15.69.

For his part, Gross couldn't have been more gracious, saying, "I just ran out of gas. That was a really hot race. It was an honorable defeat."

All of us on the Athens relay team knew about that 1984 relay. We also knew that, going into that 2004 Olympic 800 relay final, the Australians were riding a seven-year winning streak. They had won three straight world titles and had broken the world record five times. In Sydney, they had beaten our American team by more than five seconds.

In Sydney, Klete swam the anchor. He had slipped from second to fifth, then powered back in the final lap to second again, touching just six-hundredths ahead of van den Hoogenband and the Dutch, Hoogie swimming the fastest 200 relay leg ever, 1:44.88.

In Athens, Klete was going to swim the anchor again. The Aussie anchor: Thorpe. The Dutch hadn't qualified for the final. So, just as it was in 1984, everyone knew this was a two-team race, this time the Americans and the Aussies. And, as in 1984, our plan was to give our anchor as big a lead as we could. Klete had taken nearly three-quarters of a second off his lifetime best in the 200 the night before, in the Race of the Century, and still had come in fourth, behind Hoogie and me, 1.42 seconds behind Ian.

So Klete knew all too well what Ian could do. But we all knew from that Sydney relay what Klete could do, too.

I was named to swim the lead leg. Lochte pulled the second, Peter Vanderkaay the third. Just as we were set to walk out to the deck from the ready room, I said, "Wait. Come back." The four of us huddled together. "I don't know if you remember the scene in *Miracle* before the Soviet game where Brooks tells the team, 'This is your time.' Well, this is our time. I don't care what happened in the past. This is us. This is now."

I swam that first leg against Hackett. These were the Olympics, sure. But in a way it was just like it had been the year before at our little training camp in Australia. Just he and I. He turned one-hundredth ahead at 50; I moved ahead by a tenth at 100; then by three-tenths at 150; then I really turned it on. I swam that last lap in 26.78 and hit the wall in 1:46.49. The lead: 1.01 seconds. Ryan held the lead. Then Peter swam the best 200 time of his life to get us through 600 meters in 5:21.80. Klete dove in with a lead of 1.48 seconds.

Ian made it all up in the first 50. He and Klete seemed to be in a dead heat.

On the blocks, at the other end, Ryan, Peter, and I were jumping and screaming. Ian kept surging; Klete kept holding him off, barely. At 150, Klete turned first. I looked over at our team in the athlete seating area—there was Vendt on his feet, screaming, too. Jon and Bob were standing nearby. Jon knew it already even if the rest of us didn't. "If he didn't catch him there," Jon said, referring to Ian, "he's not catching him."

And he didn't. Klete got Ian at the final wall by thirteen-hundredths.

Leaning forward there on the deck, I couldn't tell immediately who had gotten whom at the wall. I had to look up at the scoreboard, and there it was, the 1 on the line that said United States. I had always been fairly reserved in my victory celebrations, especially on the world stage, but at that instant I couldn't help it and didn't want to; I raised both index fingers to the stars and let loose a scream of joy that seemed to have no end. Ryan was pumped, too. Peter, as reserved as they get, was bouncing up and down. I reached down to congratulate Klete. He, too, was usually a study in reserve. This was as excited as I'd ever seen him. He yelled, "Yeah, we did it! We kicked their butts!"

Ian, dejected, stayed in the pool a very long time. Finally, he hoisted himself up and came over to where the four of us Americans had huddled around each other in intense excitement and happiness. He waited patiently, then shook hands and walked away. It was his first 800 relay loss in international competition. The Aussie streak was done. We had finished in 7:07.33, the Aussies in 7.07.46.

It was, for me, until the 400 relay in Beijing, the most exciting moment I had ever been a part of on a pool deck. That night in Athens, I had trouble going to sleep. I kept playing the tape of the race in my head, over and over and over again.

•　　•　　•

In Melbourne in 2007, the four of us—me, Ryan, Peter, Klete—not only swam the 800 relay again, we lowered the world record the Aussies had set in 2001 in Fukuoka. They had gone 7:04.66. We went 7:03.24.

We knew the time in Beijing could be faster.

The thinking in most quarters was that it would be faster because of the suit: the Speedo LZR Racer. The suit that most of us on the American team raced in at the 2008 Olympics.

The suit was not the only reason we knew the time could be faster. But all of us spent untold hours answering questions about the suit beforehand, at the Trials and at the Games, because the suit had taken the swimming world by storm.

The full-body LZR was a major step forward in swimsuit design. It was made of special water-repellent fabrics. Built into it, to hold your stomach and lower back tight, was a corsetlike compression unit. To reduce drag, the suit had no stitches; instead, the pieces were ultrasonically bonded together. Even the zipper was bonded into the suit to help keep the surface as smooth as possible.

NASA scientists helped develop the LZR. So did, among others, Bob and I. We made a trip after those 2007 worlds in Melbourne to the Australian capital, Canberra, to what's called the Australian Institute of Sport, to do some testing before it was introduced publicly, checking where the hot points were in the suit, what happened to it when you dove in, what it felt like in it.

It feels like wearing a girdle, or at least what I imagine wearing a girdle would have to feel like. It sucks everything in. It compresses everything. It's tight around your neck. You definitely had to get used to it, and you saw a lot of swimmers reach for the zipper in the back as soon as they were done racing because it was so tight.

The suit first got noticed in a big way at the 2008 short-course world championships in England. Swimmers wearing the LZR set seventeen world records.

Lochte, who set a handful of those records, then said, "When I put it on, people joke around about this, but I feel like I'm some kind of action hero, like ready to take on the world. That's just when I put it on. It makes me feel like when I dive in that water like I'm swimming downhill."

Then came controversy, with swimmers and coaches who were not tied to Speedo wondering whether it was unfair. It was not. The suit was available for anybody and everybody. Any single person in the world could wear the suit. Speedo made it available for anybody, and as the months went along some other companies said it would be okay if their swimmers wanted to wear the LZR at the Olympics, too.

Alberto Castagnetti, the coach of the Italian swim team, may have done more than anyone else to make the controversy what it was. He called the LZR "technological doping." Still, when he came several weeks later to the U.S. Trials, he was quietly exploring whether it might be possible for any of his swimmers to wear the LZR Racer.

I was watching ESPN's *Pardon the Interruption* on one of my breaks during the Trials, and laughed when I saw that one of the upcoming topics was the suit. It got to the point where, at every press conference, we were asked about the suit.

Even Spitz, who swam in a brief and without goggles, the way it was done back in the day, got asked about the suit. Working in a reference to me, he said at the Trials, "I said this sort of tongue-in-cheek, that if that suit had hair on it, Michael would set world records in it and everyone else would get in the same type of suit. I don't really think it's the swimming suit, and if it was the suit then I am going out and buying Tiger Woods' golf clubs, because it means no matter who the swinger is, I am going to be able to score like that."

Maybe the best line of all came from Markus Rogan of Austria, a 2004 two-time silver medalist in the backstroke. Markus went to high school in suburban Washington, D.C., then to college at Stanford. He said, "I tested it. I threw it in the pool and it didn't move at all. So I'll still have to swim."

A lot of hard work went into the suit. But the suit helped make a difference of a hundred or a tenth of a second. That was not going to get our relay team under seven minutes.

This was, though: It was an Olympic year. Everyone everywhere was training for the Games. That's why times were dropping and records falling.

• • •

The Olympic record, going into the prelims, stood at 7:07.05, set by the Aussies in Sydney in 2000. That lasted as long as it took for Walters, Berens, Vendt, and Keller to swim. They finished in 7:04.66.

As it was within the 400 relay prelims, there was a competition within the competition itself in the 800 prelims—the fastest guy of the four would get to swim in the finals.

Here's how it broke down:

Walters, swimming the first leg, went 1:46.57.

Berens, second, 1:45.47.

Vendt, 1:47.11.

Keller, 1:45.51.

Erik, at that time, was definitely not going to swim in the finals. It was disappointing for him, I'm sure, because it was for me. But what was there to say? Nothing. If we won gold in the final, he would get a gold, too. That would speak volumes.

The coaches had a tough decision to make. Ricky was four-hundredths faster than Klete. But Klete had abundantly proven himself, especially in that Athens 800 relay.

Swimming is a tough sport. There's little if any room for sentiment. All anyone looking at the situation had to do was to think back to what the U.S. coaches faced in Sydney, when Chad Carvin swam in the 800 relay prelims. If anyone was deserving of extra consideration, it had to be Chad. Before Atlanta and 1996, he was considered a virtual lock for a gold medal or two; then, though, his times began to creep up. He couldn't figure out why.

He became so depressed he attempted suicide by swallowing sleeping pills. In the hospital afterward, doctors discovered why he had gotten slower—a heart condition. Chad watched the first day of the 1996 Trials in tears. He rededicated himself and was diagnosed with a degenerative back problem. Again, he came back. At the 2000 Trials, finally, he earned his spot on the team in the 400 free and in the 800 relay. In Sydney, he didn't have it the way he had hoped. He finished sixth in the 400 free, seven seconds back. And then he could not convince the U.S. coaches that he deserved one of the spots in the relay finals.

One of those spots, instead, went to an incoming college freshman who in the prelims had gone faster than Chad: Klete Keller.

Ricky had gone fastest in the 2008 prelims. So, just as it was for Klete eight years ago, now it was for Ricky. Ricky got the spot in the finals.

The rest of us knew Klete, sure. But we also knew Ricky was swimming fast and, if you swim a time, you're going to be on the relay. Just as I deserved to be on that 400 free relay in Athens, Ricky had earned his spot. Klete handled it this time around with graciousness.

Not to sound cocky by any means but, as a team, we knew going into the 800 relay finals that we were going to win. We had won this relay easily in Melbourne; no single country was close at that meet to our times, and no evidence had surfaced since that anyone was going to be close; this was not a situation like Athens in any way. The only way we weren't going to win was if someone was disqualified for a false start.

But could we break seven minutes?

I knew going into this final that I was going to swim fast. For one thing, I had not gone as fast in the 200 fly as I'd wanted to because of the equipment malfunction; this relay was the next place to prove what I still had in me. For another, when I lead off a relay, I want to help my teammates by giving them open water; if they have open water, they're going to swim faster. Thirdly, I

175

had not done what I'd wanted in my leadoff leg in the 800 relay at the Melbourne worlds; I had wanted to back up the 1:43.86 I'd had there in the open 200 with a similar swim but, instead, went a full second and a half slower, 1:45.36.

I was still mad about that.

And then, looking up into the stands, we saw several of the stars of the U.S. Olympic basketball team, including Kobe Bryant, LeBron James, Chris Paul, Jason Kidd, and Carmelo Anthony. No way were we giving it anything less than 100 percent with those guys on hand to watch. On deck, we could even hear them cheering. That was cool, those guys cheering for us.

I was fired up when I dove in. It showed, too. I went 1:43.31, the second-fastest time of all time. We had a lead of more than two seconds when I touched, Ryan—then Ricky, then Peter—looking at nothing but open water ahead.

I swam in the relay with the same pair of goggles that hadn't worked in the 200 fly. They didn't work right in the relay, either; one side filled up a little bit. But this time I could still see.

Back on the deck through Ryan's swim, I was encouraging Ricky to step it up. "When you have a guy like that yelling at you, you better do what he says," Ricky said later.

As Peter made the final turn of his four laps, we had already thrown down such a dominating performance that the camera had to pan back to the left just to get the other swimmers in the picture. "Come on!" I yelled at him. "Let's go!" And go he did. When he touched, the scoreboard said 6:58.56.

We had not just gone under seven minutes; we had gone a full second under seven. We had put four guys together who wanted to achieve a common goal, who had the talent and the confidence to achieve that goal, and this race showed what we could do together. Of all the records broken in Beijing, this race was the one in which we lowered the record by the largest margin, 4.28 seconds.

Inevitably, the reporters afterward wanted to know whether the other guys were swimming in part for me. Peter put it best. He said, "I think it's special to be a part of that, but there's still a ton of pressure on us to win, anyway. We want to win. We want to do it for the U.S.A. and for the team. I don't think there's much more pressure than there already was."

The gold medal was my fifth in Beijing, the eleventh of my career. The media crews naturally wanted to know what I had to say about that. "You're always an Olympic gold medalist," I said. "Birthdays happen every year. Christmas happens every year. You only go to be an Olympic gold medalist so many times and it definitely never, ever gets old—you know, listening to the national anthem play with a gold medal around your neck, it's one of the greatest feelings I've ever had in the sport of swimming."

To keep it going, meanwhile, I was clearly going to have to get a new pair of Speedo Speed Socket metallic goggles. I borrowed a pair from Ricky. He was done competing. As for me: six swims still to go, three of the six finals: the 200 IM, the 100 fly, and the medley relay. Eleven swims were in the books. And I still felt very, very solid.

6

COURAGE:
THE 200 INDIVIDUAL MEDLEY

Whether it was at the pool or in the village, my teammates would not and did not talk to me about eight gold medals, in much the same way that a pitcher's teammates avoid talking to him during a no-hitter or a perfect game.

At night, in our suite in the village, we would play cards or the board game Risk. We'd talk about anything but swimming. Just guy stuff. The games were supercompetitive. One night Lochte and I, playing spades against Cullen and Eric Shanteau, found ourselves down 385–5. The game was to 500; we came back to win. There was lots of hollering and carrying on.

You would never have known that Shanteau had been diagnosed with testicular cancer. Which is just the way he wanted it.

At the 2004 Trials, Eric had finished third in both the 200 and 400 IMs. He hung in there. In Omaha, he made it onto the 2008 team, in the 200 breaststroke. At training camp in Palo Alto, he told us he had competed at the Trials knowing he had been diagnosed; the tests had come back on June 19, about a week before the start of the Trials. Eric had talked it over with the doctors and they had given him their okay, he could go to Beijing. Surgery could wait until after the Games.

Eric told us all these things at a team meeting after we had finished dinner, taken a team photo, and filed back into a meeting room. Everyone was getting drowsy. Then Eddie stood up and said Eric had something to say. And then we were all, like, oh, my God, what do you say? Fortunately, Eric had the words: "I've been going through this for a while now and it's not the easiest thing. But I've been able to get the okay for being here, and trying to accomplish my goals and dreams."

That wasn't all to the story, either. Eric's dad, Rick, had been diagnosed with lung cancer the year before.

I hadn't known Eric that well before Beijing. He is an awesome guy. The whole time we were at the Olympics, he was fully alive, fully living his dream. Ultimately, he didn't win a medal, but who cared?

I admired the way Eric was handling the challenge. Just as I was motivated by Dara Torres, who proved over and over again that age was no barrier to anything, winning three silver medals in Beijing, and by her coach, Michael Lohberg, who had been diagnosed with a rare blood disorder, aplastic anemia, after the Trials but before we flew to Asia. Just as I had been deeply affected by the fight against cancer of a boy in Baltimore who had become a good friend, Stevie Hansen.

The day after the 200 fly and the 800 relay, I had no finals—I swam the 200 IM semifinals in the morning, the 100 fly prelims at night—and so I had, for the first time since the Games had begun, a moment or two to reflect on the struggles, the journeys, and the courage of people I knew and what it meant to be a hero.

The five gold medals I had won had already prompted so much talk about me being a hero. After the fifth medal, the president of the International Olympic Committee, Dr. Rogge, had called me "the icon of the Games." He also said, "The Olympic Games live around super-heroes. You had Jesse Owens. You had Paavo Nurmi, Carl Lewis, and now you have Phelps. And that's what we need to have."

Castagnetti, the Italian coach who had stirred so much talk about the LZR, said I was "undisputedly the greatest swimmer of all time." He had a unique perspective; like Spitz, he had competed at the 1972 Olympics in Munich.

There was funny talk about science fiction. After the 800 free relay, Alexander Sukhorukov of Russia, with a silver medal around his neck, said, "He is just a normal person but maybe from a different planet." Cornel Marculescu, the executive director of FINA, said something very similar: "The problem is, we have an extraterrestrial. No one else can win." British swimmer Simon Burnett said something much like that, too, talking with Eddie Reese when they ran into each other in the cafeteria. "He was saying to me, 'I think I've figured out Michael Phelps,'" Eddie said later. "'He is not from another planet. He is from the future. His father made him and made a time machine. Sixty years from now, he is an average swimmer but he has come back here to mop up.'"

I would find out later that there were other stories in which I would be described as the greatest American athlete of our generation, or comparing me to the likes of Michael Jordan or Tiger Woods. On NBC, Dan Hicks, who called the swim races from the Water Cube, had described me as "Tiger in a Speedo."

All these comparisons were humbling. To even be mentioned in the same sentence with some of the greatest, most dominating athletes in the world was overwhelming, especially because I was just doing what I love to do. My goal was never to become the best athlete ever; it was simply to become the best athlete I could be.

If what I was doing was helping inspire someone else to stand up and take on a challenge, I was honored by that.

But a hero?

Stevie Hansen was a hero.

Stevie was only seven when he was diagnosed with a brain tumor, in October 2002. He was a promising age-group swimmer; at six, he was not only already swimming but winning awards.

The day before Stevie's surgery, I brought over a flag, some shirts, and a poster. We shot hoops in the driveway at his house and we just talked about how each of us loved to eat junk food. The day of the surgery, I made sure to send balloons to the hospital. Stevie's dad, Steve Hansen, later told me that meant the world to Stevie.

It made me happy to try to make Stevie happy, that's all. This is the way my mom raised me. This is the way I am. If Stevie had wanted to meet me because he thought I was a cool swimmer, I quickly came to learn that he was a cool swimmer, too, and a brave, even fearless, young man.

Over the next year, Stevie seemed to get better. That next summer, I sent a note saying I wanted to come watch Stevie swim at a local meet. Which I did. I showed up unannounced. When he saw me, Stevie sprinted over, leapt into my arms, and said, "Wow, you came!" I got to watch Stevie that afternoon as he raced in the free, the fly, and the relay. We had lunch together and I signed autographs for the other kids, including Stevie's sister, Grace, who never lets me forget that I used a red Sharpie on her forehead. I then got persuaded to swim a relay leg myself in a parents' and coaches' race, even though I had to borrow a suit. Stevie was thrilled. I was thrilled for him.

Throughout the 2004 Olympics, and after I came back and moved to Ann Arbor, I made sure to stay in touch with Stevie and the Hansens as he underwent three more surgeries. So, in April 2007, when Stevie's mom, Betsy, called my mom, to say, "We have a disaster here . . . he wants to see Michael," there was no question.

I rearranged my schedule to get to Baltimore. Then I had one of those days traveling that everyone seems to have at one point. The plane was late. Bags were lost. So, by the time Mom and I got to the Hansens' house it was already after midnight.

We stayed there for two hours, maybe longer. Stevie was only eleven and so desperately ill. But his fighting spirit, that's what had always impressed me about him. I sat there on Stevie's bed, holding his hand, just talking. He was sound asleep and didn't wake up. Even so, I was sure he could hear, which is just what Stevie told his mom the next morning: "I wish I had woken up. But I know he was here."

The next day, I posted a note to Stevie's personal page on an Internet site for people confronting serious illnesses. I said, "Stevie, it was great to see you last night. I'm really glad I got to visit. You are very brave. You really are an inspiration to us all. Talk to you soon—Michael."

"Yours was a gift like none other," Betsy posted back.

Stevie died on May 29, 2007. The memorial service took place a few days later. I sent purple flowers—purple was Stevie's favorite color—and I was honored to be asked to stand with the Hansens as they greeted friends and family.

I was sure Stevie was looking down on us. I was just as sure that, when I went to Beijing, Stevie was cheering from above.

Stevie had told his parents he wanted me to try to win an Olympic medal for him. At his bedside that night, just a few weeks before Stevie passed away, I made Stevie this promise: I'd try to get a medal. Hopefully, it would be gold.

• • •

I owed Stevie my very best effort in everything I did at these Olympics. And the 200 IM was going to take every bit of that effort. Just like the 400, it demands consistency and endurance across all four strokes. And just like the 400, it exposes flaws or weaknesses, only faster.

I had not lost in the 200 IM, at least in a 50-meter pool, in a major competition. Lochte had gotten me at the end of 2007, at the short-course nationals, but that was just weeks after I'd broken my wrist.

I had no intention of losing at the Olympics.

The top four seeds in the Beijing final were the same top four going into the final in Athens: me, Lochte, Laszlo Cseh, and Thiago Pereira of Brazil. In 2004, though I got the gold, my winning time was well off the world record; I pushed the pace but simply didn't have the physical strength to get home over the final 100 meters. By that point in my Athens schedule, I was probably more worn down than I knew, and you could see that the polish and pop in my stroke was just not there.

This time I had no doubt. It would be there. I was going to take it out hard early, like the 200 free, and dare the other guys to match what I could do.

Laszlo sat on my shoulder through the first 100, through the fly and the back, and even into the turn for the breast. Maybe I would flinch? No chance. I reeled off far and away the fastest breast split of the top four, 33.5, a second faster than Laszlo, more than a half-second faster than Ryan. Coming off the 150 turn, I was already a body length ahead of Laszlo.

This time, I could drive hard for the finish. My last lap: 27.33. Nobody else even broke 28.

I touched in 1:54.23, 57-hundredths of a second better than the 1:54.8 world record I had gone in Omaha.

Laszlo was second, Ryan third. Both those guys went faster in Beijing than I went for gold in Athens; even so, I had touched more than two seconds ahead of each of them. When the results went up on the big board, I reached over to Ryan's lane; we shook hands and patted each other on the head.

Ryan's bronze has, in some quarters, been overlooked, too. No way should it be—and this is no knock on Laszlo, who earned the silver. Laszlo, in fact, was the definition of sportsmanship after the 200 IM, saying, "It's not a shame to be beaten by a better one."

Ryan, meanwhile, tackled one of the toughest doubles imaginable that morning. At 10:19 that morning, he swam the 200 backstroke final, winning gold and setting a world record in defeating Aaron Peirsol, among others. The 200 IM final went off at 10:48. Ryan only had twenty-seven minutes in between the two races. For him to medal in both races was just amazing. Only he and another American, John Naber, have ever done it, John in 1976 in Montreal.

Later, on the medals stand for the 200 IM, Ryan and I got to smile and enjoy what we'd done, but just for the briefest of moments. Now, it was my turn to double, twenty-nine minutes from the end of the IM until the semifinals of the 100 fly. As soon as the anthem was over and some photos taken, I switched from my dress sweats to my parka and shoes, I threw my cap and goggles on, and then they pushed us out there. The medal from the 200 IM—I was now six-for-six, twelve career golds, fourteen overall—was in my warmup jacket.

• • •

After I won that sixth gold, I was asked in a news conference, "What do you say to those who think you may be too good to be true?"

I wasn't surprised by the question.

If anything, I was only surprised that the issue of doping hadn't come up until this point in the Games.

"Anyone can say whatever they want," I replied. "I know, for me, I am clean. I purposely wanted to do more tests to prove it. People can say what they want, but the facts are the facts."

I knew going into Beijing that anything I might do there, any medals I might win, would without doubt be viewed by some with skepticism. Doping scandals will do that, and, in recent years, there had been far too many doping scandals in sports. Since I had won my medals in Athens, the Mitchell Report had fallen upon baseball. Floyd Landis had failed a doping test and had his 2006

Tour de France victory taken away. Marion Jones, who had won five Olympic medals in track and field in Sydney, was sentenced to federal prison at the beginning of 2008 for lying to federal agents about her use of performance-enhancing substances.

So, I understood why there might well be skepticism. Somebody somewhere does something and immediately the first reaction now is, well, he or she is on the juice. It might be unfair, but it's reality.

I wanted to help do something to help change that reality.

I understand that kids look up to athletes. If any kid anywhere was looking up to me, I never, ever would want to let that young person down. Growing up, I watched the Olympics. I watched Cal Ripken, Jr., play baseball. I looked up to Michael Jordan, too. I watched all these great athletes compete for the love of the game, because they were having fun. That's what I wanted to do, too.

When I was younger, I proved I could do without Ritalin. Then, in ninth grade, I did a school project on drug cheats, at about the time I started to be tested myself, when I was fourteen and just onto the national radar. Then, later in high school, I saw how devastating it could be for someone to be accused of doping. When Beth Botsford, the North Baltimore swimmer, grew up, she became engaged to Kicker Vencill, another swimmer. In January 2003, an out-of-competition doping test found evidence in Kicker's system of a by-product of the banned steroid nandrolone. Kicker told everyone he was innocent. A nutritional supplement he was taking, a multivitamin, must have been tainted, he said, and there was good reason to believe this was very likely what had happened. In 2001, an IOC-financed study had found that 15 percent of the hundreds of products tested contained steroid precursors, a building block that the body turns into steroids, even though the precursors weren't listed anywhere on the label. The contamination might happen during the manufacturing process, might be the fault of tainted ingredients. Doesn't matter. The rules of international sports are that if something is in your system, it doesn't matter how it got there; it doesn't matter in the slightest whether you intended to cheat. All that matters is if it's there. Ignorance is never an excuse. Kicker was banned from competition for two years. Later he went to trial, and in a California court won a jury verdict against the vitamin manufacturer; after that, the case settled. But Kicker's Olympic dream was ended.

There are two kinds of doping tests. Some you take at a competition; you know you're going to get tested if you're at a big meet and, usually, one of the top finishers. Other tests are unannounced. That is, if you're on the testing lists, which are kept by the U.S. Anti-Doping Agency and by FINA, a tester can show up at the pool or even at your house—anywhere, really—and order you to take a test, right then and there. You have to keep USADA and FINA notified at all times of your whereabouts. If you don't agree to take the test, it counts as a positive.

The rules are strict, but they have to be.

The rules for Olympic athletes are much, much stricter than they are for NFL players or Major League Baseball players. That's not fair, but those of us who are not cheating, who would never cheat, have learned to embrace the double standard, not get mad about it.

In fact, we have tried to make the contrast even more clear. At the start of 2008, USADA was putting together a project in which twelve U.S. Olympic athletes would volunteer for extra testing: not just urine tests but blood as well, six weeks of tests, once a week, to establish a baseline. If USADA asked, your entire medical history would have to be provided. It all went toward going as far as possible to answering the common-sense question: What would you do if you knew you were clean?

I heard about this project from Dara, who said she was going to do it.

I wanted in, too. I wanted to prove to everybody that I was 100 percent clean.

Ultimately, USADA picked three of us swimmers among the twelve—Dara, Natalie Coughlin, and me. The others included track and field stars such as Bryan Clay, who would go on to win gold in the decathlon at Beijing.

I willingly provided the extra samples, even though the first time, when they took five vials of blood from me, I confess I felt a little woozy afterward. Five vials is a lot of blood.

From early June through the end of the Olympics, I was tested probably twenty-five to thirty times. I was tested every day at the Trials and at the Games. The day I checked into the Olympic Village, I was tested.

I'm clean. Always have been, always will be. Facts are facts.

7

WILL:
THE 100 FLY

Of the seven medals that Matt Biondi won at the 1988 Olympics in Seoul, five were gold, one was silver, and one bronze.

Matt's silver came in the 100 fly. Matt was first at the turn and with 10 meters to go was still in the lead. As he neared the wall, though, Matt got caught between strokes. What to do? He opted to glide instead of taking an extra stroke with his arms, even if that extra stroke might have been nothing more than a half stroke. The problem: Matt was father away from the wall and the touch pad than he thought.

At 99 meters Matt was in first.

At 100 meters he was in second. Matt's glide allowed Anthony Nesty to sneak past. Anthony was timed in 53 seconds flat, Matt in 53.01.

Anthony was a sophomore at the University of Florida who was swimming for the country in which he had grown up, Suriname, a small nation on the northeast coast of South America.

The entire country had one 50-meter pool. For three years prior to those 1988 Games, Anthony had been training in the United States, first at a private school in Jacksonville, then in college in Gainesville.

Suddenly, Anthony was indisputably Suriname's first-ever Olympic medalist. He was also the first black man to win an Olympic swimming medal. In Suriname, they would go on to issue a stamp in Anthony's honor, as well as commemorative gold and silver coins.

Initially, Matt could not believe what had happened. "One one-hundredth of a second," he said afterward. "What if I had grown my fingernails longer?"

In 2002, at the nationals in Fort Lauderdale, after I out-touched Ian Crocker for my first major victory in the 100 fly, Anthony came up to me and said, "That's how I beat Matt Biondi in the 100 fly that day. It was the touch."

That day was the first time I truly understood how important the finish of the 100 fly could be. Among all the events on my race schedule, the 100 fly was always going to be one of the hardest, if not outright the most difficult, of the individual races. Why? Because, compared to the others, it is much shorter, a simple up-and-back sprint. And because my habit of swimming the first 50 at easy speed and then coming on hard was always going to leave me fighting at the end.

When I was twelve, Bob shocked me one day. We were at a meet and he said, Michael, you know what my job is?

No, I said.

It's to get you in the ballpark.

You know what your job is?

It's to get your freaking hand on the wall. And he didn't say freaking.

Bob was trying, even then, to drill into my head that a finish was important, that you swim aggressively all the way to the wall. He would not tolerate lazy finishes in practices, ever.

It all came together that day in 2002. Just hearing Anthony say it made real what Bob had been preaching. If I nailed the touch, it could make all the difference.

I thought about all of that in Beijing after hustling through my semifinal swim in the 100 fly.

Milorad Cavic of Serbia looked strong. He and I had been in the same preliminary heat the day before. In that prelim, he had turned first and finished in 50.76, an Olympic record; I was sixth at the turn, a body length behind, but predictably surged the last 50, closing to finish second in 50.87. In the semis, Cavic got through with the fastest time; I was second-fastest; Crocker, since 2003 the world-record holder in the event, was tied for third, with Andrew Lauterstein of Australia, and said, "People point at me, but Cavic is looking good and it'll be a tight race."

The final was indeed going to be tough. I needed to try to be faster in the first 50 and come on even stronger at the finish. The touch might make all the difference.

•　　•　　•

"On this planet," a Korean journalist had asked me in a news conference in the middle of my week of racing in Beijing, "is there anybody who can defeat you? And if so, who is it?"

I laughed and shrugged: "I don't know."

A moment or two later, I said, "I'm not unbeatable. No one's unbeatable. Everyone can be beaten."

Ian Crocker had beaten me before in the 100 fly. And though we had become good friends, he wouldn't be all broken up if he were to beat me in Beijing. Not in the slightest.

"Sports is all about one person trying to derail the other person's dreams," Crock said. "It's kind of the dog-eat-dog part of sports. Michael has his goals and I have mine. I'm not going to feel bad if I race my heart out and end up winning."

Crock is one of the greatest athletes ever to come out of the state of Maine. And Maine didn't even have it as good as Suriname when Crock was growing up; in the entire state, there wasn't one Olympic-sized pool. Instead, Crock spent his first training years swimming in a four-lane, 25-yard pool attached to an elementary school; the pool was also used to provide therapy for the developmentally disabled. As Crock tells the story, their diapers didn't always work.

Crock, like me, was diagnosed with a learning disability, in his case attention-deficit disorder. In high school, moreover, he began developing signs of depression; when he went away to college, to Texas, he sought help and was prescribed the antidepression medication Zoloft. Then he was able to kick the medication cold turkey.

Crock has always been one of the most thoughtful guys out there, a guy with insight and perspective. He has for years had a thing for classic cars; one of the first cars he bought was a 1971 Buick Riviera. He got his first guitar in the eighth grade, for Christmas. Asked to name his favorite Bob Dylan tune, he says it's like asking him to choose among which of the breaths he has taken over the past twenty-five years. His blog quotes from Steve Earle's "Fort Worth Blues," its lines about the highway:

> *It's just the only place a man can go*
> *When he don't know where he's travelin' to.*

Not surprisingly, Crock has a certain way with words. "The 100 fly is the gift I was given," he said. "So, you shake your money-maker . . . and you see what happens."

Crock won the 100 fly at the 2000 Trials. In Sydney, he finished fourth, 22-hundredths of a second away from bronze; he also swam the final of the gold medal-winning, world record-setting medley relay. By 2002, I had added the 100 fly to my program; in Fort Lauderdale, I beat him and went under his American record. That set the stage for the next year, and the Worlds in Barcelona.

In the first of the two semifinals in Spain in 2003, Andriy Serdinov of the Ukraine went 51.76, lowering a world record that had stood for five years. He got to hold the record for as long as it took me to swim the second semi. I went 51.47.

In the final, I went 51.10. I had lowered the record again. But Crock went 50.98. He was the first man under 51.

In the warm-down pool, Bob offered a two-part lesson: Let the loss go. And think fast now about how, having come up just short, you're going to present yourself to reporters. Are you a sore loser? Or are you gracious? Remember, he said, better here than next summer.

"I hate to lose and I think it's going to drive me even more," I said when I met the press. "It definitely makes me hungrier for next year leading into Athens. I have a lot of goals for that meet and I think the 100 fly is a big part of that."

There was more to winning in the 100 fly, meanwhile, than just that race. The fastest American in the 100 fly also earns a spot in the finals of the medley relay. Second-best got the prelim, and I was suddenly in the prelim. Bob was adamant: I was going to swim in that prelim. It was my responsibility.

I went home from Barcelona with five gold medals but, as well, the image in my mind of Crock and the three other guys on top of the podium after winning the medley in record time.

Crock had prepared better for the 100 fly in Barcelona than I had. He had executed better than I had. If I was going to turn that around in Athens, I had to do better.

The morning after the 100 final, a local paper ran the headline, "Phelps es Humano." Translation: "Phelps is Human."

• • •

The headline on the cover of the October 2003, issue of *Swimming World,* in bright yellow letters, shouted, "Super Flyer." That would be Crock, guitar in hand, leaned up against that

1971 Buick. Inside was a lengthy feature that included a center-fold of Crock swimming the fly. I ripped out that centerfold and plastered it on the wall above my bed. Every morning, the first thing I'd see when I woke up was that photo. Every morning that photo was a kick in the backside. It drove me. It pushed me. It punished me.

At the 2004 Trials, Crock not only beat me again, he lowered his world record, to 50.76. The Olympic final was shaping up to be a classic.

By then, thanks to numerous stories about what I'd done with the poster, he knew full well that he was motivating me. But, it turned out, I was motivating him, too. He had in his head the image of me rushing by him on the final 50, and he didn't like that one bit.

We were, in the best spirit of what sports is supposed to be all about, pushing each other to be the best each of us could be.

The 100 fly semis in Athens turned out to be a rerun of sorts of Barcelona. Serdinov won the first semi, in an Olympic record, 51.74. In the next semifinal, I went him one better, 51.61. Crock went 51.83.

The medley relay heats took place before the 100 fly final. Thus, the coaches had to make a decision that ended with me swimming in the heats. Crock had beaten me at the Trials and in Barcelona; he had to be considered a slight favorite for the 100 fly finals. Plus, earlier in the week he hadn't been at his best physically, and that had showed in the 400 free relay; better to rest him for the 100 final.

Did I want to swim in the medley finals? "Big time," I told the press. "Everybody wants to swim in the finals of a relay. I missed out on that last year, and I really want to do it here."

As I was warming up before the finals, Bob looked me over. He liked what he saw, liked the look in my eyes. Michael's going to win, he thought.

At the turn, however, it looked like I was doomed. Crock got off the blocks like a rocket. At the turn he was under world-record place; I was in fifth, 77-hundredths of a second behind him.

As I hit the wall, I turned the power on. I surged into third, Serdinov and Crock still ahead.

In the stands, Bob had stopped looking at the pool at 50 meters, figuring I was too far back. At 20 meters, I had pulled up to Crock's shoulder. At 15 meters, Bob looked down again at the water. Well, he thought, second isn't that bad.

The three of us churned toward the wall. Serdinov, though, bobbed too high and Crock got caught in midstroke while I timed my strokes perfectly. I reached for the wall at full extension, at the end of my stroke, just as I was supposed to do.

My goggles came off so I could see the scoreboard.

Serdinov, it said, had touched in 51.36.

Crocker: 51.29.

Me: 51.25.

Seventeen races into my program in Athens, and I still had enough in me to reach for the wall and my dreams. Four-hundredths of a second—the touch could, indeed, make all the difference.

Crock said on television, "Michael is just pure tough. That's like just the only word for it. So, I mean, I knew he was going to be tough. And I just got out there and gave it my best shot. And I'm real proud of both of us."

Later, on a victory lap, in the stands I saw Spitz. He waved to me, his thumb down, the other four fingers up, a sign he knew full well what I had done. The 100 fly was my fourth individual gold in Athens, the same number of individual medals he had won in Munich.

I also had the two bronze medals, of course, in the 200 free and the 400 relay. And I still had the medley relay to go, which, assuming the American team won, would make it eight overall.

Crock, on the other hand, came to Athens anticipating three golds. If I swam the medley final, he would go home with none.

Before I started swimming the 100 fly, Crock had been the undisputed best in that event. Now I was Olympic champion. But, because of me, he was now the world-record holder.

Crock had a silver and a bronze at the Olympics. How could that seem like failure? And yet, somehow, it did. Why did he have to have gotten a sore throat at the Olympics, of all times? It wasn't right. It just didn't seem fair for a guy who, for as many times as I had looked at his photo, was someone for whom I had developed abundant and profound respect. He was rival and competitor, yes. But also my teammate and my friend.

I thought about this some more, then told Bob that Crock could have my spot in the medley final. He deserved it, I said.

Okay, he said. He understood. Go tell Eddie, Bob said.

"Michael," Eddie said, "are you sure this is what you want? It has to come from you."

"It is."

Someone else went to tell Crock, who was coming out of drug testing, to get back in the pool for another warm-down swim. But I'm done, Ian said. No, he was told, no, you're not.

Now it was his turn to say no. I didn't earn it, he said. But you deserve it, we said.

Eventually, he agreed. We let Eddie make the announcement to the press. I said, and I meant every word, "We came in as a team and we're going to go out as a team." Crock said, "I'm kind of speechless. I feel like it's a huge gift that is difficult to accept but it makes me want to just go out and tear up the pool."

Which, of course, he and the other three guys—Peirsol, Hansen, Lezak—did. Crock turned in the fastest butterfly split ever in the medley and the American team took nearly a second off the world record. I got to wear baggy shorts and flip-flops and lead the cheers from the stands.

After the medal ceremony, Crock came over to where I was sitting. We hugged each other.

"Congratulations," I said.

196

"Thank you," he said.

Later, Crock told everyone, "I thanked him because he was one of the main reasons I had the opportunity to do that. He gave me a gift."

It was an easy call, really. It was the right thing to do.

•   •   •

After those Games, of course, Crock and Krayzelburg and I criss-crossed the country on our tour. We were with each other twenty-four hours a day for several weeks. Crock opened up and we had a good time in each other's company. A documentary film, *Unfiltered*, shot in the months between Athens and the 2005 Worlds in Montreal, chronicled it all.

When the tour ended, Crock got back to serious training. Me? I endured the ferocious anxiety of my back problems, got arrested for drinking and driving, moved to Ann Arbor, and had to learn how to live life away from home. Other distractions abounded as well. I made the rounds of various talk shows. I judged a beauty pageant.

At the 2005 Worlds in Montreal, Crock thrashed me in the 100 fly. Absolutely dominated. He not only beat me by more than a second, he lowered the world record—his—to 50.4.

When I saw Bob afterward, I said, "I want to put a bag over my head."

He looked at me and said, "Me, too."

Immediately after those Worlds, I was off to China, on a promotional tour arranged by some of my sponsors. Finally, in September, Bob had had enough.

"Michael," he said, "what is it you want to do? What are we doing here?"

"I want to swim all my events," I said. "And I want to win."

"You know what needs to happen?"

"I know."

I did, in fact, know. I just needed to hear myself say it.

The 2007 worlds in Melbourne were not all that far away, in late March of that year, after a long Australian summer. I knew what needed to happen.

In all of 2006, Crock and I went head to head only once, at the summer nationals. I won, touching in 51.51, Crock in 51.73. The nationals served as the qualifier for the Pan Pacs; I passed in Victoria on the 100 fly, Crock going on to an easy win, 51.47, in the finals.

The 100 fly final at the 2007 Worlds took place on a Saturday night. By the time we stepped onto the blocks, I had already won five golds at the meet. This race could be six. The 400 IM, seven. The medley relay, eight. Crock got to the turn first, with me third. We tore for the final wall and, again, I caught him at the end, if just barely, touching in 50.77, Crock in 50.82.

Five-hundredths of a second.

In Athens, I'd won by four-hundredths.

"Knowing that he's having the meet of his life, I expected him to go very fast and he did," Crock said afterward. "I'm just glad I still hold the world record."

"That's how I won the Olympic medal," I told the reporters. "You have to nail the finish as best you can."

The very next morning, Sunday, April 1, brought the medley relay prelims. Crock, as the silver medalist in the 100 fly, was up third on the blocks for the butterfly leg, swimming with Lochte, Scott Usher, and Neil Walker. Those guys put up what would have been the fastest time overall by more than two seconds. Except, on the board next to United States, it said DSQ. Disqualified. Crock had left the starting block too soon.

The rules allow a relay swimmer the leeway to start three-hundredths of a second early. Crock, according to the timing device, had gone off four-hundredths before Neil touched, meaning his feet had left the blocks one-hundredth of a second too fast. When the judges ruled against him, Crock slapped his hands to his face in disbelief.

A few hours later, he stood up at a team meeting in our hotel and apologized. I didn't mean it, he said. I feel horrible. He kept talking about how bad he felt.

I knew Crock didn't purposely false-start. It was a mistake; people make mistakes. There was nothing I could do. It happened. I could win seven medals in Melbourne, not eight. Crock apologized. It was over.

At least from my perspective, it was.

But as 2007 rolled into 2008, Crock didn't seem himself.

At the U.S. nationals in Indianapolis in the summer of 2007, Crock false-started again, in the 100 fly; I ended up winning the event. A photographic strobe had mistakenly been fired after the "take your mark" command but before the beep; Crock flinched.

In Omaha, in the prelims of the 100 free, Crock false-started yet again.

It wasn't only that I won the 100 fly at the Trials, Crock coming in second. It's that I beat him by 73-hundredths of a second. He wasn't, for whatever reason, himself. In the prelims in Beijing, he inexplicably wore a jammer, a suit that runs from the waist to just above the knees; his time was so poor he almost didn't make the semifinals. He switched back to a legsuit for the semifinals and swam much faster, tied for the third-best time with Lauterstein, the Australian.

You could tell when Crock was on and when he was not, and I wanted him on. When he was on, he had speed, he had tempo. I like racing people at their best, and I knew that through the Trials and even into the prelims and semis of the Games he was not at his best.

Then again, he might have that one special race still left in him.

• • •

And then there was Cavic, Milorad on the scoreboard, Mike to all of us who had known him for years, a guy who had been born in Southern California, went to high school there, then to college at

Berkeley. Cavic had been training in South Florida with Mike Bottom, who used to be the coach at Cal and had proven himself time and again as one of the best anywhere at developing sprinters; Bottom was in Florida with a bunch of guys—Gary Hall, Jr., Nathan Adrian, and others—that was called "The Race Club."

At the Olympics, Cavic was swimming for Serbia in part because he could. Each country gets two entrants per event. To qualify at the U.S. Trials in the 100 fly, Cavic would have had to have gotten by me, Crocker, Stovall, Tarwater, and others.

Not to say that he didn't have talent. Cavic had ability. He finished sixth in the 100 fly in Melbourne, for instance. In Beijing, he had put up the sixth-fastest time in the prelims of the 100 free, proving he was on his game, then scratched out of the semifinal to concentrate on the 100 fly.

Before 2008, though, Cavic had never shown that he was a breakthrough talent on the Olympic stage. His Olympic run in Athens had ended in the semifinals of the 100 fly when water had flooded the inside of his racing suit. After that, he dealt with back problems, even taking several months off in 2006.

He did, however, have a talent for getting noticed.

In the prelims at big meets, the fastest swimmers are seeded into the last three heats. The early heats, and at a meet like the 2007 worlds there are sixteen heats, are for swimmers who are expected to go much slower. In heat number one of the sixteen 100 fly heats in Melbourne, however, there was Cavic; the start list didn't show a qualifying time next to his name. The only two others due to swim in that heat were a guy from Ghana and another from Malaysia. And then the guy from Ghana didn't go. So, Cavic essentially had open water, which is always an advantage. The three fastest times from all 16 heats in those prelims: Crocker, 51.44; Cavic, 51.7; me, 51.95.

At the European swimming championships in March 2008, Cavic was suspended for wearing a T-shirt that proclaimed, in the Serbian language, "Kosovo is Serbia," as he was awarded his gold medal for winning the 50-meter butterfly. After that, he went to Belgrade, where he was greeted by hundreds of fans and met with the prime minister, who called him a "hero."

Because of that suspension, Cavic didn't get to swim the 100 fly at the European championships. Thus he came to Beijing slightly under the radar.

After setting the top time in the semifinals in Beijing, Cavic did not simply allow the time to speak for itself. Instead, he said:

"I've got nothing against Michael Phelps. The guy's the king. Do I want to make a rivalry of this? Of course. Why not?"

And: "It would be kind of nice that one day, historically, we'll speak of Michael Phelps maybe winning seven gold medals, and having lost an opportunity to win eight gold medals. When they talk about that, they'll talk about whoever that guy is that took it away from him. I'd love to be that guy.

"I think it'd be good for the sport, and it'd be good for him if he lost once. Just once.

"Let's be honest about that. It's true. It's good to lose sometimes. I know because I've lost a lot. For him, what would it mean? I would hope that he would cut down on his events for the next year and start training more for the 100 fly. There's no doubt in my mind that he's the best. Will he be the best here? I don't know. He's got a lot on his plate. Hopefully, that will work out for me."

Gary Hall, Jr.—the same Gary Hall, Jr., who made so much noise in 2004 about me being on the relay—predicted in the *Los Angeles Times* that Cavic would beat me. After training with Cavic at The Race Club for a year and a half, Gary said, Cavic had "worked harder than anyone," had "endured taunt and torment from his teammates, myself included, for being overzealous with his training," adding, "We caught him sneaking in extra workouts."

Gary also said in that article that Cavic had "matured a lot, had somehow mellowed in the right ways and matured in others," had "become something of a champion and a team leader," adding, "He never faltered."

Gary closed his piece by recounting a toast he had made in Cavic's honor: " 'Here's to the guy that is going to upset Michael Phelps in the 100-meter butterfly,' I said, handing him his Race Club–embroidered terry cloth robe at the team dinner at the end of the season before heading off to the Olympic Trials.

"It looks like for once I might be right."

During the heats, Cavic made a shooting motion, as though his hand were a gun. He was asked if he had been "shooting" at me over in the next lane. "That's ridiculous," he said. "If you were there, you would have seen I was firing above him, at my manager."

I had no idea at the time that any of this was going on. I didn't know the first thing about it until, at breakfast the morning of the final, Bob said to me, hey, Cavic says it would be good for swimming if you got beat and he'd love to be the guy who took the gold medal away from you.

I perked right up. What?!

• • •

We walked out onto the deck with the Water Cube roaring with noise. In the stands, just up off the blocks, my mom sat between my sisters, Hilary on her right, Whitney on her left. They were holding hands, tense.

I was in Lane 5, Crocker 6, Cavic 4. As I went through my pre-race routine, stretching, I turned in Cavic's direction; he was turned to face me. It looked to a lot of people, including Bob, as if he was trying to stare me down, which, later, Cavic denied, saying of me, "Maybe he was able to see to see the reflection of himself and he's like, 'Hey, I look pretty good.' I saw myself in his reflection and was keeping things under control."

Bob absolutely, positively thought Cavic was trying to play

mind games with me. I had no idea. I saw him looking in my direction, and looked away. I was looking out through my metallic goggles in his direction, but not at him. I was paying no attention to what he was doing. Why would I? Bob had always instilled in me this notion: What does Tiger Woods do? What did Michael Jordan do? The great champions—there's nobody on their level, he used to tell me, and so when they're competing they're competing against themselves, and only themselves. You hear Woods talk after a great round, Bob would say, and what does he say? Something like, "I had good control of my game today," or, "I managed the last five holes really well." Never anything like, "Gee, I was really worried whether I was going to beat Vijay, or Ernie, or Phil." You be like that, Michael, Bob would say.

The goal in this Olympic final that Bob and I had sketched out was for me to turn at 50 meters at 23-point-something seconds. If you turn at 24.2, Bob said, you're dead. At 24-flat, he made plain, well, you'd be making it very difficult on yourself but you might still have a chance.

My goal sheet for this race had me finishing at 49.5. No one had ever gone under 50 seconds. Crock's world record had been at 50.4 since 2005.

The goal sheet, it turned out, was perhaps too aggressive. Everything else about this race, though, was unbelievable.

"Take your marks," the big voice boomed out over the Cube. Beep!

The dive. The underwater. Just as I had visualized it.

I popped up and launched into the fly. Fluid, strong, easy. Cavic, I knew, would be going out faster than I was. Crocker, too. I wasn't particularly worried. They had their style, going out harder on the front half; I had mine.

Hilary couldn't stand it any longer. She stood up on her chair. Behind her was a woman from Holland; the Dutch woman kept pulling at her shirt and yelling, "Sit down! Sit down!" Hilary turned and yelled back "I'm watching my brother and I'm going to stand. He's a good swimmer and you're going to have to tackle me if you want me to sit down!"

Bob, over on the other side of the stands, was imploring me to go faster: "Come on! Come on!"

At 50, I wanted to be half a body length back. I looked at the turn and saw Crocker and thought, okay, Cavic's not too far ahead.

What I didn't know was that I was seventh at the turn, in 24.04.

Cavic had turned first, at 23.42; Crock was right behind him, at 23.7.

Halfway down the backstretch, as I passed Crock to my right, I moved up on Cavic, to my left.

The Dutch woman was still pulling on Hilary's shirt: "Sit down!" Mom was fretting out loud, talking to Hilary, to Whitney, to no one and everyone, hoping against hope that what she was saying wasn't really going to come true, that just saying it might make it not happen: "He's going to get second. He's going to get second."

With 15 to go, Cavic knew I was coming hard. He said later he saw "kind of a shadow by the side of my goggle," adding, "The last 15 meters, the last eight meters, I just put my head down. I did not breathe the last eight meters. I was just hoping for the best."

In the coach's box, Bob was swaying like he was at a church service. Left, right, left, right.

In the water, Cavic and I hurtled toward the wall together.

Cavic opted to glide in.

I chopped my last stroke. It was short and fast, a half-stroke, really. I still can't fully explain why. Maybe it was experience. Absolutely competitive will. There wasn't time, really, to form a complete thought. It was an impulse. I knew I had to do something. The situation demanded action. Gliding was not going to win gold. It didn't for Matt Biondi and it for sure wasn't going to for me.

The Omega timing pads take roughly 6.5 pounds of pressure—3 kilograms—to trigger. Anything less and the pad thinks it's just waves and won't respond. Anything that much or more, you turn off the clock.

Both Cavic and I touched, turned, and looked at the scoreboard.

Next to my name, it said: 1.

I looked over to where Bob had to be, pointed that way with my left hand, slapped the water with both hands and roared in victory, Olympic champion again, four years ago by four-hundredths of a second, now by one-hundredth, the smallest margin there was or ever could be. Mark Spitz had won seven medals at a single Olympics; now, with stupendously hard work, ferocious willpower, and a little luck, so had I.

In that instant, I had just matched the great Spitz.

At the finish, Bob initially thought I had lost. He muttered, a note of dejection in his voice, referring first to Cavic, then to me, "Oh, he got him." Then Bob swiveled to his right, to take in the board. In that instant he went from the lowest of lows to the highest of highs: "Oh! Oh, my God! Oh, my God!"

As Cavic and I had driven toward the wall, my mom had put up two fingers, for second. As we hit the wall, Hilary, still standing, still screaming, had her left arm around Mom. The two of them looked up at the board and Hilary started shouting, "Oh, my God! Oh, my God! Oh, my God! He won, he won, he won!" Mom just stared in disbelief. Hilary said, again, "He won!"

Mom sunk down into the chair as if she didn't have any bones. She was numb. Stunned.

Hilary and Whitney and everyone around them were going nuts, jumping up and down, shaking, freaking out, Hilary yelling over and again, "I can't believe it!"

In the pool, I said to Cavic, "Nice job."

Then I turned to Crocker. He and I shook hands and hugged. I leaned back, right elbow on the deck and lifted my left hand in the air, wagging just one finger high above me.

First, in 50.58 seconds, a flash of history in the present tense and proof that no matter what you set your imagination to, anything can happen if you dream as big as you can dream.

Cavic touched in 50.59. Lauterstein was third, in 51.12. Crocker was fourth, out of the medals, in 51.13, by one-hundredth of a second.

•   •   •

The close finish drew a formal protest from the Serbian team. Officials from FINA, the international swimming federation, said video replay confirmed what the scoreboard said.

The issue was never going to be whether Cavic ought to be the winner and me the runner-up, according to Cornel Marculescu, executive director of FINA. It was, he told reporters afterward, whether the race ought to be called a tie. FINA officials reviewed the video evidence frame by frame, and the race referee, Ben Ekumbo of Kenya, said, "It was very clear the Serbian swimmer had second, after Michael Phelps. It is evident from the video that it was an issue of stroking. One was stroking, the other was gliding." To make sure everyone was on the same page, FINA officials shared with the Serbian team the video evidence; if the Serbs had not been satisfied, they could have taken the protest to an appeal jury. Instead, Marculescu said, they were satisfied that I'd won and Cavic had come in second.

Cavic wore his silver medal to a news conference and said, referring to the race, "I'm stoked with what happened. I'm very, very happy."

Before the race, as Bob told me, Cavic had a lot to say. Afterward, Cavic had a lot more to say. At that news conference, he said, "Perhaps I was the only guy at this competition who had a real shot at beating Phelps one-on-one. This is completely new to me; I've never been in such a position with so much pressure, and I am very proud of how I handled that whole race and how I was able to keep myself under control emotionally and the stress level. It is a frightening thing to know that you're racing Michael Phelps, but I think that it's even more frightening to know that it's going to be a very, very close race and that nobody knows the outcome.

". . . I read a lot of articles online. I like to read—it encourages me and I knew a lot of people had their money against me. That was totally understandable. Michael has been breaking world records here by seconds. This is something that no other swimmer in swimming really does, so what do you expect from a man who breaks world records by seconds in the 100 fly? You know, I expected that he'd go a world-record time—maybe something close, like 50.2. But it was a real honor for me to be able to race with Michael Phelps and be in this situation where all eyes were on me as the one man that would possibly be able to do it. It was just great.

"Pieter van den Hoogenband talked to me yesterday and I told him, 'Pieter, this is pretty stressful. I'm scared. I don't know what to expect.' And he just said, 'Just enjoy the experience, just have fun, and don't get too nervous. This is a beautiful thing.' Just hearing this from a legend such as Pieter—it really kind of calmed me down and I was like, 'He was right, the best races I've swum, I've swum when I was relaxed.'

"I believe I just did that here."

Asked about the appeal, he said, "You know, people will be asking me this for years, and I am sure people will be bringing this up for years, saying that, 'You won that race.' Well, you know, this is just what the results showed. This is what the electronic board showed. I guess I kind of have mixed emotions about it, you know. This could be kind of the where—if I had lost by a tenth of a second or two-tenths of a second, I could probably be a lot cooler about this but with a hundredth of a second I'll have a lot more people really saying that, 'You know, you won that race.' That kind of makes me feel good, but I'm gonna be happy with where I am."

The very last question of Cavic's news conference went like this:

"In your mind, was Michael Phelps the gold-medal winner?"

"Uh, is Michael Phelps the gold-medal winner? He— I think if we got to do this again, I'd win."

My style, as ever, was to let my swimming do the talking for me. Besides, there would never, ever be an "again." The time to seize that moment was right then, right there.

When I chopped the last stroke, I thought at first that it cost me the race. But it turned out to be just the exact opposite. If I had glided, I would have been way too long, caught in what swimmers call just that, a long finish, the way Cavic was. Instead, I turned a long finish into a short finish. I knew that little extra half stroke had to be a quick stroke, fast as I could do it.

I did some highly technical little things right at the very end, too, which Cavic did not, and those bought me time and made a difference. My head was down; his came up. My feet were straight; his, again, came up. Swimming fast is, generally speaking, a horizontal proposition; vertical movements slow you down. It typically pays to be in as straight and horizontal a line as possible. I was. He wasn't.

After the race, my mom and my sisters got to come on deck for just a moment.

"We're so proud of you!" came the chorus. Mom had that glowing, adoring look that only mothers looking at their children can have. That look doesn't change when the kids get to be big kids.

I let them in on a secret: "I didn't realize I was that far behind."

Still on the deck, I was put on the phone with Spitz, who was back in the States. "Epic," he told me. "What you did tonight was epic. It was epic for the whole world to see how great you are."

He also said, "When I look at Michael and I think of the lore of what he has done over the last four years—it's more remarkable than myself." The two others with nine gold medals over an Olympic career were, as it turned out, in Beijing. Carl Lewis said, "The reality is, congratulations." Larisa Latynina, the Soviet-era gymnast, wrote me a note that said, "You have shattered all sort of records with truly inspiring Olympic character." It also said, "In ceding my record for most Olympic gold medals, I do it with little regret. I am sure we share the joy of competition and a timeless joy for excellence."

Earlier in the week, I had said when asked about being "the greatest athlete in Olympic history," that I was "kind of at a loss for words." I explained, "Growing up, I always wanted to be an Olympian, and now to be the most decorated Olympian of all time, it just sounds weird saying it. I have absolutely nothing to say. I'm speechless." Now I had won seven and, no matter how many times I was asked, I still felt as if I was at a loss for just the right thing to say. I tried to explain my feelings this way: "I knew that in my dreams I always wanted it, and thought that under perfect circumstances I could do it. Just believing all along that you can do it goes a long way."

Maybe a little something extra helps, too—what Crock told me after the race. I'll never forget it. He said, marveling that I had somehow pulled it off, "You have to have angels with you, or something."

8

COMMITMENT:
THE MEDLEY RELAY

No one could have been more supportive of my swimming for Mark Spitz's records than Mark Spitz.

Mark showed up in Omaha near the end of the 2008 Trials to take in the scene, and to tell anyone who would listen his emphatic prediction: I would win eight gold medals in Beijing.

"This is going to be history," he declared. "He's going to do—what we say—a little schooling to the rest of the world, and it's going to be exciting for those that will see it in person and for those who watch it on TV."

Mark also said that he had only good feelings about the possibility of seeing someone else in the record books on the line that says, "Most Golds Won at One Edition of Olympic Games, Individual." He said, "Records are made to be broken," adding, "Thirty-six years is a long time."

He also said, sitting at the head table in a room off the warm-down pool in the Qwest Center, dozens of journalists scribbling down everything he had to say, "It just dawned on me that it was forty years ago that I was at training camp, and I was going, wow, that is almost twice as old as Michael Phelps is now! Wow, I swam a long time ago and, it's okay, it's okay."

I first met Mark in 2004, at the Trials in Long Beach, not until then, as improbable as that may seem in hindsight. I knew he was likely to show up at some point at those Trials —Mark is based in Southern California—but didn't know until after I won the 200 fly that Mark would be presenting nineteen-year-old me with the medal for the victory. At the podium, Mark shook my hand and leaned in to say a few words: "I'll be over in Athens to watch you, and I'm behind you all the way. I know what you're going through. I went through it once before. Enjoy it. Have fun with it. Go get 'em." Mark has always had a gift for the dramatic and at that point he hopped onto the podium, grabbed my right wrist with his left hand and raised both of our arms to the sky. He then pointed to me with his right finger, as if to say, here's your new champion. It was, and is still, one of the most exciting memories swimming could ever have given me.

When I won six golds in Athens, Mark remained steadfastly encouraging. It was hardly a failure to win six gold medals, he would remind anyone who asked. Just wait, he would say. Michael is going to be better in 2008 than he was in 2004.

Through the years, Mark could also not have been more gracious in pointing out how swimming had changed from his time to mine. In 1972, swimming featured a semifinal round only for 100-meter events; in each of Mark's 200-meter events, he had to swim twice for a gold medal. I had to swim three times for each individual gold, with the exception of the 400 IM, an event with no semifinal. Over the course of the meet in Munich, Mark swam thirteen times in eight days, in all about 1,800 meters of racing, just over a mile; in Beijing, I would swim seventeen times over nine days for 3,400 meters, or just over two miles. In Mark's day,

American swimmers had very little international competition, and the relays, in particular, were all but guaranteed United States wins; by 2008, swimming was definitely global. The proof: In Beijing, swimmers from twenty-one countries would ultimately win medals. Moreover, Mark was not only the first to win seven golds; he was the first to win six. Going into Munich, he didn't have to deal with the same sort of media attention—not to mention that the media world in 1972 was not one filled with cable channels, Internet outlets, newspapers, magazines, all of which had a never-ending need for copy and outtakes. "I can unequivocally say he has shown a different type of courage than perhaps I did," Mark said of me. "I was not chasing Mark Spitz's record."

In Omaha, it was hardly surprising to see that Mark would show extraordinary insight about what awaited me in Beijing, his remarks almost foretelling the challenges in races such as the 100 fly: "There were so many things that had to go right with my story with each one of my events, and there is something that had to go wrong with someone else. So they didn't get that one flash of the greatest swim of their life to beat me. And it is kind of scary when you think about it, because it could have happened in any of the events."

He also ticked off three concerns that might stop me from getting to eight:

I obviously had to win the first event, the 400 IM. That I had done.

I had to continue my "winning ways" in the 100 fly, which he, like most observers, had tagged as the single toughest individual event on my calendar, in part because it was the one event in Beijing I would be racing in which I was not the world-record holder.

I had won the 100 fly.

Finally, Mark said, Michael can't control the relays, adding, "Anything can happen."

On paper, the medley relay, the final race of the Games at the Water Cube, looked like we should—repeat, should—win. But the Aussies had improved enough in their individual 100s to make a lot of people nervous. When you added up their best flat-start times in the four disciplines and compared them to ours, the Aussies were within 43-hundredths of a second, even if their best times had come in the semifinals, ours in the finals. Bob told my mom before the race that he thought our chances of winning were 60–40, maybe 70–30.

This was a relay the United States had never lost at the Olympics (not counting the Games in 1980 in Moscow, when the U.S. team didn't take part). The four of us in the finals—Peirsol, Hansen, me, Lezak—had been swimming medleys together since the 2002 Pan Pacs in Yokohama, when we set a world record. The 2004 team, with Crock swimming the butterfly leg in the finals, had won gold; Crock took the butterfly leg in the prelims of the medley in Beijing, so he stood to win gold again if we won in the finals.

And I was going for an eighth gold.

But that last element was not the be-all, end-all. "We absolutely respect and admire Michael's goals but the feeling on the team is that by no means does one man come first," Aaron told the *New York Times* before the medley final.

"Honestly, when Lezak pushed out that relay, the next day guys were bringing up the fact that if Lezak didn't touch out, Mike might not have had his eight golds. It's not something Mike talks about. No one here is racing for second place, even the guys racing Mike. The feeling on our team is, we're all racing to win. He's doing exceptionally well; we're all rooting for him. But by no means is he the only one we're rooting for."

All the U.S. coaches were nervous. Everyone knew how much was at stake.

Safe starts, they kept saying. Safe starts. If we heard it once we heard it a dozen times: If your start is a tenth too slow, you can make it up; if it's a tenth too fast, you're done. It's an awful feeling, we kept hearing, to swim wondering if you'd false-started.

Crock made sure in the preliminary to start safely, if cautiously. "When Phelps is done, I don't want to stand in the way, to do something stupid like '07," he told a reporter later. "I want him to have every shot he's got."

Grevers, who swam the backstroke leg in the prelim, acknowledged everyone's anxiety: "I don't think we were going to leave China if anyone DQ'd us," he said.

The morning of the final, the Cube was so jam-packed, with attendance way past the announced capacity of about 17,000, that people were crammed four and five deep in the aisles. Kobe Bryant and LeBron James came back to root us on. Our teammates and coaches were there. My family, of course—Whitney in a gold-colored top, Hilary a gold jacket, both in gold on purpose. Mom opted for black, nervous as always before the start of the race. On deck, there wasn't much to say; we'd do any talking afterward.

I was more than fired up. I'd gotten a text message that morning from back home, from Troy Pusateri. When I was just starting out at North Baltimore, Troy was one of the older boys; he used to call me "Little Phelps." Troy was always himself mentally tough, too; he went on to become a Navy SEAL. Of all the messages I got from home during the course of the 2008 Olympics, Troy's is the only one I saved so that I could read it afterward, get fired way, way up time and again. This is what it said:

"All right, brother man!! Last race!! This one is NOT for you . . . it's for your fans, like me, who you inspire every day for the past six years . . . it's for Bob and your mom. . . . for without them none of this would be possible . . . it's for the United States . . . the best damn country on the face of the earth . . . it's for history!! It's for you making this sport what it is today!! It's for all the people who talked smack and doubted you ever!! It's for being the best Olympic athlete ever to grace this planet!!! Go get 'em!! Don't hold back!! You can do it, buddy!! I'm so damn proud of ya!! Give 'em hellllllllll !!!!!"

On the deck, we got ourselves ready as Aaron and the other backstrokers got into the water and got set to go. The individual medley starts with the butterfly; the medley relay starts with the backstroke, which only makes sense. If backstroke were not first, the starting backstroke swimmer and the finishing previous swimmer might well crash into each other.

Beep! Aaron and the others dove backwards, arms above their heads, and the race was on. The quiet of the start gave way to an immediate wall of sound all around us.

Aaron had won gold in the 100 back in both Athens and Beijing. His backstroke is elegant. And yet still so powerful. He got us off to a solid start, though, as it turned out, he was 62-hundredths of a second slower than his gold-medal swim earlier in the week. Fortunately, Australia's Hayden Stoeckel was 83-hundredths slower than the lifetime best he went in the 100 back semifinals.

Brendan went next. His time was respectable, 59.27, but he was passed by both Kosuke Kitajima of Japan—his 58-flat split the fastest of all time—and by Australia's Brenton Rickard. We were in third when it was my turn. The Japanese didn't have the speed in the third and fourth legs, so they were not much of a worry. So it was now me and Lauterstein—a rematch of sorts from the 100 fly the day before.

My start was deliberately super-slow. It was, in fact, so slow I actually saw Brendan's hands touch the wall. I was taking no chances.

Lauterstein got to the wall first but I just hammered hard on the turn. When I came up from underwater, I was in front. This was my last swim of the Games. I gave it everything I had. Everything.

I drove so hard that my finish was ugly. Caught between strokes again. This time I did glide. Had to.

When I touched, though, Jason had a cushion of 81-hundredths of a second.

In the seventeenth of my seventeen swims, even with that glide slowing me down, I laid down the fastest 100 fly leg in history, 50.15; Lauterstein's split of 51.03 was even faster than his 51.12 flat-swim for bronze the day before—but factoring in a relay flying start, not as fast as we had thought he might go. No way Jason was going to let himself, us, the United States down. He dug hard to the far wall. He turned and dug harder for home.

As soon as I touched, I sprinted out of the pool to watch the race from behind our block. The noise level in the building was now out of control. Except for the guys in the water, it seemed everyone in the building was yelling. I was excited beyond words but also calmly confident. About halfway through Jason's final lap, it became clear, even obvious—we were going to win. Standing there on the deck, I knew it. In the stands, Bob knew it, too. Eamon Sullivan was coming hard, but Jason was holding him off.

With 15 meters to go, Bob thought to himself—you know what, this is actually going to happen. They're going to win and Michael is going to have eight medals. He's not going to have seven; he's really going to have eight.

"Come on, Jason!" Mom was yelling. "Come on, Jason! Come on, Jason! Come on, Jason! Come on, Jason!"

Jason came home strong, and as he touched with his left hand, the roar of history enveloping all of us, my mom yelling, "Yes!" long and loud, holding the note as if she would never let it end, I pumped my fist in triumph, then grabbed Aaron and shouted, "Let's go! Let's go!"

Jason pulled himself up out of the water and we huddled, just the four of us. "We're part of history," he said. Jason had gone

46.76 to Sullivan's 46.65; we had won by seven-tenths of a second; we had set a new world record, 3:29.34. I said, "Without what you guys just did for me as a team this whole week, none of this would have been possible. We worked as a team and we worked really well together. I want to thank you guys for the opportunity you gave me."

In the stands, fate had put Ian Thorpe in the row immediately ahead of Mom and my sisters. He turned around and wished them congratulations, saying graciously and sincerely, "Good job. That was great."

Mom cried and cried, tears of joy and relief and amazement.

We were honored after the race to be able to carry around an American flag that had flown in Iraq; it had been sent to one of our teammates, Larsen Jensen, a bronze medalist in Beijing in the 400 free. It made a special moment that much more special.

When the medals ceremony ended, walking along the side of the pool, I saw Mom and the girls and started climbing through the photographers to get to them. The photographers parted, allowed me to get to my mother and sisters, then, as if on cue, immediately closed in around us. Surrounded there by dozens if not hundreds of cameras, by thousands of fans still packed into the Water Cube, it nonetheless seemed as if we were in our own little bubble.

I said, "I'm so tired."

•　　•　　•

Brendan won two breaststroke medals in Athens. In 2006, he set three world records in breaststroke events in three weeks. In Omaha at the 2008 Trials, he won the 100 breast. Then, to the surprise of many of us, he finished fourth in the 200 breast, failing to qualify in that event. What he did thereafter speaks to the kind of guy Brendan is. He immediately said he would try to help the two guys who beat him in the 200, Shanteau and Scott Spann. And then, when he could have begged off, Brendan went to sign autographs and pose for photos at a session USA Swimming had organized.

The 100 breast final came early in the week in Beijing, on Monday, overshadowed completely by the 400 free relay final an hour later. Brendan, who is not related to my friend Stevie's family, finished fourth. What Brendan did after that underscored again what kind of guy he is. He ran into my mom at the Beijing version of USA House, a gathering spot for the USOC and for American athletes and guests at every Olympics, and vowed, "I'll be ready for the relay."

Brendan was not at his greatest in the medley. But, as he promised, he was ready. He did his part. And what he said after the race made plain why anyone would be proud to call Brendan a teammate.

"It's one of the greatest things sport in general has ever seen," Brendan said when asked about the eight medals. "I mean, coming from a swimmer, looking at what he did, there's an immeasurable amount of respect for what he did. The shame of it is other athletes are not going to realize how hard what he did is.

"The world is fast at swimming now. The world was not fast when Mark Spitz did his seven. Everybody is stepping up. Michael got on the blocks for every final against seven different people and denied them every single time. That just goes to show—it's every part of sport. It's endurance, it's strength, it's pressure.

". . . He made the pressure putt in the U.S. Open, he won the Tour de France, and he knocked out the best fighter in the world in the sixteenth round with an uppercut. He did absolutely everything sport is supposed to be and he did it with a smile on his face, and he's a good kid."

Brendan had another great line that, when I read it later, I also truly enjoyed. He said he had been amazed that I could separate myself so seemingly completely from the pool when I wasn't at the Cube. Brendan said, "I'd be like, 'Do you realize what you're doing?' And he'd be like, 'Man, the pizza is good today.'"

Aaron and Jason had great words, too.

Aaron said, "He's coined a new term: the Phelpsian feat. We've all heard of the Spitzian feat. I think there's a new one now." Jason said, "Before the race, I saw Kobe and LeBron, the two best players in the world in basketball. I love basketball; there is no way I was going to let these guys down. They came out here to watch this—it was awesome."

Seemingly everyone around the pool, in the moments after the race, was suddenly fair game: What do you think of what Michael did? Some of the answers were hugely, hugely flattering. Like Leisel Jones, the Australian breaststroke champion, who won two gold medals in Beijing: "I couldn't care less about my swims. To swim the same era as him has been awesome." Or the Australian coach, Alan Thompson: "We've been talking about Mark Spitz for thirty-six years now. I don't know if I'm going to be alive when they stop talking about this bloke. You wonder if we are going to see someone as good as this again."

I got whisked to a news conference in the basement of the Water Cube. In those moments after we'd won the medley, it dawned on me that my life had abruptly moved into a new and completely different phase. President Bush called, and said, "If you can handle eight gold medals, you can handle anything." I'd been told that our medley swim had been shown on the big screens at M&T Bank Stadium in Baltimore after the Ravens faced the Minnesota Vikings in a preseason NFL game; more than 10,000 people stayed to watch us win. The Associated Press had filed a "flash" onto the wire when the medley ended with us winning; the AP uses a "flash" only for what it believes is a "transcendent development," which through the years has meant such occasions as the shooting of President Kennedy, the first moon landing, the falling of the Twin Towers.

And now—for swimming.

I was, as I said in my first comments at this news conference— held in a basement of the Water Cube, the room hot and sweaty, packed beyond full with reporters and cameras—"fairly speech-less." I tried to explain: "This is all a dream come true," seeing as my main goal was to raise the sport of swimming as "high as I can get it." Besides the Ravens game, I said, I'd heard they had made an announcement at Yankee Stadium when I'd won the 100 fly. The St. Louis Cardinals had held up their team bus back to the hotel in Cincinnati so the players and coaches could watch us win the medley. "People all over the place are saying it's crazy. They're out to eat, the TV is on and swimming is on. I think the goal that I have and I'm working toward is in progress . . . I think it's really just starting to get more of an awareness for the sport in the United States. By far, it's already starting. It started four years ago. With the help of my team and the coaching staff, I think this sport can take off even more than it is. That's a goal that isn't going to happen overnight. It's going to happen over time and that's something I'm going to be in the long run for."

I tried, too, to explain why my emotions surfaced so much more in Beijing, there for everybody to see on live television, than they had in Athens: "I've dreamed of a lot of things. I've written down a lot of goals; this was the biggest one I ever really wrote down. Sort of thinking of all the memories I've had through my career to get here, with my family, my friends, my coaches—my coach, I've really only had one coach—everything I've gone through. It's—I guess my mom and I still joke about it, I was in middle school and I had a teacher say I'd never be successful. It's little things like that. It's stuff like that you think back to and it's just fun. I saw my mom for a minute and we just hugged. She started to cry. I started crying. My sisters started crying. It has been a really fun week and I'm really glad to accomplish everything I wanted to."

After that news conference, Bob and I were whisked away to another one, to a much bigger room at what was called the Main Press Center a few minutes away from the Water Cube. By then, Darryl Seibel, the USOC's chief communications officer, had joined us. He had been through these kinds of media get-togethers a time or two before and knew just what to say.

"Are you hungry?" he asked me.

"God, yes."

"Cheeseburgers?"

"God, yes."

Darryl sent a USOC volunteer to the McDonald's in the press center for four cheeseburgers and fries, pronto. When the burgers arrived, Bob knocked back one in world-record time and I wolfed two.

Before we went out to meet the press again, I cleared my BlackBerry again of yet another avalanche of e-mails and text messages. I would clear it; it would fill up immediately; I would try to clear it; I'd get a new batch. I couldn't keep up.

When we walked out onto the stage of the room at the press center for this next news conference, it was even clearer to me just how my life was changed. This room was enormous. It was crowded beyond capacity, too.

One reporter wanted to know if I had stayed in the Olympic Village or a fancy hotel. The village, of course, I said. I got to meet Rafael Nadal; he was one of my favorite tennis players to watch on television. I saw Roger Federer. I saw Dirk Nowitzki, I said.

What about Spitz? "Being able to have something like that to shoot for made those days when I was tired and I didn't want to be there—you wanted to go home and sleep instead of work out—you look at him and you say, 'I want to do this.' It has been something I wanted to do and I'm just thankful for having him do what he did."

Mostly, I said, I was just thankful.

For the way it had all worked out: "Seeing 8/8/08 and the opening ceremonies starting at eight, I guess it was maybe meant to be. I don't know. For this to happen, everything had to fall into perfect place."

For my teammates. For all the games of spades and Risk at

night. The laughs we shared. "I just wanted to make sure I took every single moment in and every single swim in, every single moment with my teammates, so I would remember them. I don't want to forget anything that happened."

For my family, and for Bob. Bob said, "Clearly, an accomplishment of this magnitude doesn't happen with just one or two people. There are a lot of people who have been involved in this process, from Michael's family, my family for that matter, everyone back at NBAC where we started and will soon return, all our fans in Ann Arbor and Baltimore, Club Wolverine—I'd like to thank them for everything they've done. And particularly this amazing Olympic swimming team, the best group of guys I've ever been around—and it has just been an honor to be a part of it."

For sure, I planned to be back at the Games in 2012, I said, but probably doing different events.

When that press conference wrapped up, we went across the street to the NBC compound at what was called the International Broadcast Center, to Dick Ebersol's office. There, for the first time since arriving in Beijing, I got to spend more than just a moment with my family. President Bush had given me a message for my mom: Hug her for me, he had said. I made sure I followed the president's orders.

Bob was in the room. So was Mike Unger of USA Swimming. Peter Carlisle, Drew Johnson, and Marissa Gagnon of Octagon were there, too, along with Dan Hicks, Rowdy Gaines, Andrea Kremer, Tommy Roy, Drew Esocoff, and a few others from NBC, and, of course, Ebersol, whose office had banks of TV screens. He asked, what do you want to see? The 400 free relay, I said before he could even really get the question out.

I could watch that relay 100 times and I think I'd still have the same reaction—wow, that really happened.

We watched that relay and some other races. We saw my mom cry watching me. Hilary, too.

Dick and I had come to occupy a special place in each other's lives that had nothing to do with how many medals I won or how the broadcasts of the Olympics did in the ratings. He had supported me, stood up for my character, when I'd been called to account for drinking and driving; just a few weeks later, he was badly hurt in the plane crash near Telluride in which his son, Teddy, who was just fourteen, was killed. Mom and I were honored to be invited to the funeral. Dick had followed me as I had grown up after Athens and I had learned so much from him about what strength in the face of adversity looked like. In his eighth-grade graduation speech, Teddy had said, "The finish line is only the beginning of a whole new race."

Watching the replays, Dick cried, too.

•   •   •

That half hour in that office was one of the few moments of quiet and calm in what quickly became a whirlwind.

No complaints. None at all. The opportunities that were extended to me from around the world were unbelievably thrilling. And every single one might be the one that would encourage some little boy or girl somewhere to get to the pool to start swimming for nine medals.

Bob and I had, before the Games, come to an understanding. I would be back in the pool, just not immediately. The 2009 World Championships, in Rome, weren't until the summer; my mom had always wanted to see Rome, so I had to be back in time to try to make the team. Bob said, fine, see you in early 2009 back at the pool, back in Baltimore. He announced several months before the Olympics that he was going back to NBAC, to become chief executive officer. Starting in Rome, you might see me focus on different events: more of the sprints, for instance, maybe the 100 free, perhaps the 200 back. Both of us were excited, me to have new goals, Bob to see whether a guy more naturally suited for longer distances could make the switch. Beyond that, I fully intended to compete at the 2012 Summer Games in London, assuming I qualified for the U.S. team. My plan all along has been to be retired from swimming by the time I'm thirty; London, when I will be twenty-seven, figures to be my last go-round.

Enjoy whatever it is you're going to do, Bob made plain before we left Beijing. He didn't have to say the rest—make good decisions.

From Beijing, it was off to London, where I took part in the ceremony that marked the end of the Games and the handover from the 2008 to 2012 Summer Olympics. In Orlando, I rode in a convertible down Main Street at Disney World with Mickey Mouse. In Chicago, more than 150 of us from the 2008 U.S. Olympic team got to be on *The Oprah Winfrey Show*; I also was privileged to add my support to Chicago's bid for the 2016 Summer Olympics.

In Los Angeles, I got to be a presenter at MTV's Video Music Awards and a guest on shows such as *Jimmy Kimmel Live* and *The Tonight Show with Jay Leno.* In New York, I rang the bell, along with Lochte and Natalie Coughlin, at the New York Stock Exchange and hosted *Saturday Night Live.* On *SNL,* I got to joke that being on the show was "like, the ninth greatest moment of my life." In the audience that night was Bruce Springsteen; at a concert a couple weeks before in St. Louis he had, before launching into "Thunder Road," given me a shoutout: "Eight golds, man—whoo!" The *SNL* musical guest—the one and only Lil Wayne, whose music had gotten me in the mood before getting on the blocks in Beijing—he gave me a signed iPod that held forty unreleased tracks, one of them called "Michael Phelps," about me. I hardly knew what to say besides—thank you.

Everywhere I went I was flattered to have touched so many people. A driver in Cleveland told me, "You honored the entire country with your effort." At the baggage check-in in Newark, one of the skycaps said, "Congrats, Michael—you killed it out there."

Everywhere, it seemed, swimming had become part of the

national conversation. When the Los Angeles Angels clinched the American League West title in early September, one of their outfielders, Torii Hunter, put on goggles, got down on the floor in a pool of champagne and beer, and shouted out, "I love it. I'm Michael Phelps!"

In late September, I went back to Ann Arbor for the Wisconsin-Michigan football game and had one of those experiences that gave me chills. I saw Bob for the first time since Beijing; we got to go into the Michigan locker room before the game, where I told them to beat the Badgers. The players were all fired up and so was I, and then Bob and I walked down to the field through this long tunnel under the stadium. The Michigan band was in there, and as soon as they saw me at the top of the tunnel, they all started going nuts. As we walked toward the field, the cheers echoed in front of us and rolled out into the great bowl, and then the people outside heard what was going on, and they started applauding, and so by the time we got to the light, the entire stadium was cheering. And that was way before we were introduced, when we got another thunderous ovation.

In Baltimore the next weekend, the city formally welcomed me home with both a parade, which also honored Katie Hoff, as well as Paralympic athletes and Special Olympians, and then a fireworks show at Fort McHenry, birthplace of "The Star Spangled Banner."

All of it was amazing. It sometimes seemed surreal, especially because I never set out to be a celebrity. I set out to be the best I could be and then to do something no one else had ever done, and as we zipped from one city to the next, it was never far from my mind that, for sure in my case, celebrity comes with a certain responsibility. I was privileged enough that people wanted to hear me and see me. What was it I could tell them?

The answer, in part, came with the establishment of a foundation we set up immediately after the Games that bears my name with the aim to get kids into swimming and to help teach healthier lifestyles. I donated the entire $1 million Speedo bonus. Then Speedo and its North American licensee, The Warnaco Group, Inc., announced another $200,000 donation, and Kellogg's, which put my picture on boxes of Frosted Flakes and other products, donated another $250,000. One of the foundation's first initiatives: visits to a number of cities to launch an educational program that helps kids achieve their goals. The program is based on what my mom and Bob, in particular, helped me learn when I was younger: to set goals, take responsibility, and practice discipline.

Maybe we're onto something. By the fall, USA Swimming announced that record numbers of kids were signing up at local clubs. In Mount Laurel, New Jersey, enrollment in the learn-to-swim program doubled; in Chicago, the Lyons Swim Club saw a 28 percent increase in their team size from the beginning of August through the end of September; in Farmington, New Mexico, the Four Corners Aquatic team grew by 40 percent; in Sarasota, Florida, the YMCA Sharks added 135 new members, a 36 percent increase.

Through all the glitz and the glitter after the Games, some of my best memories will always be the quieter moments, especially those I was lucky enough to spend with kids, particularly at Boys & Girls Clubs across the country. In Burbank, California, at the Boys & Girls Club, a seven-year-old named Javier Silva gave me a handmade leather bracelet; he had put eight little gold rings on it. He told me that he had watched me swim a lot at the Olympics and that he was my number-one fan. I told him I would wear it; I was true to my word. A few days later, at the Dunlevy Milbank Community Center in Harlem, I watched a group of about two dozen boys and girls swim laps. Never, I said, let anyone tell you that anything is impossible. "There were people who said no way anyone could win eight medals," I said. "When people say that, I want to prove them wrong. I was able to prove them wrong this year. And one of the best things about the most exciting time in my life was looking up and seeing my mom there."

All over the country—really, the world—people have gravitated toward my mom. As many people, maybe more, have come up to say, "We love your mom," as have said, "Congratulations." At the close of *Saturday Night Live,* the female cast members kept saying, we love your mom—she's awesome!

She is awesome.

In early October, President Bush welcomed more than five hundred members of the 2008 U.S. Olympic and Paralympic teams to the White House. We gathered on the South Lawn and, as part of his remarks, the president said, "People say, did you ever get to meet Michael Phelps? I said I did. So that was the highlight? I said, not really. Meeting his mother was more of a highlight. She reminded me of my mother—plain-spoken and full of love."

Everywhere my mom went after the Olympics, people would stop her and say, "Hey, Debbie," hundreds, maybe thousands, of people she had never before met calling her by her first name as if they were old friends. People wanted just a moment with my mom—to say thank you, to say wow, to say what a great family we are. Mom had people tell her that the love she had for me and my sisters, and all of us for her, was something that America needed, that it was evidence of American values at their best. Mom had people stop her at the store and say, "Debbie, outstanding job—we are so proud of you and your son."

Mom also starred in one of the best stories that came out of the 2008 Summer Olympics. Mom likes to shop at a clothing store named Chico's. After she got back from Beijing, she went to her favorite Chico's and, after some parking difficulties, was approached by a security guard in the parking lot. He started talking to her. Then a flash of recognition lit his face.

"Hey," he said, "I know you. You—you're the seven-medal mama."

Mom didn't miss a beat. She said, "Eight."

ABOUT THE AUTHORS

Michael Phelps is an American swimmer. He holds the record for winning the most gold medals (eight) in a single Olympics (2008). He has won sixteen Olympic medals, fourteen gold and two bronze. He holds seven world records and has more than twenty World Championship medals.

After returning home from Beijing in 2008, Michael used the well-publicized $1 million Speedo bonus he received to start the Michael Phelps Foundation, through which he hopes to encourage children to lead healthy, active lives and to continue to grow the sport of swimming. He now resides in Baltimore, Maryland, with his dog, Herman.

Alan Abrahamson is an award-winning sportswriter and a recognized authority on the Olympics. In 2006, he left the *Los Angeles Times,* where he had been a staff writer for seventeen years, to write for the NBC suite of online properties, which now includes NBCOlympics.com, NBCSports.com, and UniversalSports.com. Since 2003, Alan has also served as a sports and Olympic analyst for the NBC television networks. Among other honors, Alan won the 2002 National Headliner Award for sports writing and was named the Los Angeles Press Club's 2004 sports journalist of the year. Alan, his wife, Laura, and their three children live in Southern California.